EARLY PRAISE FOR
Culinary Leverage

"Chef Doug Keane has written an inspiring tale of dreaming big, succeeding against all odds, and upending an industry in the process. His voice on the page is raw, humble, and darkly funny. He reminds us that a more decent world is possible. *Culinary Leverage* is riveting, courageous, and honest. I think you will enjoy it."

—Chef Jacques Pepin

It is a rare gift to know someone as talented, humble and self-aware as Chef Doug Keane. In the two decades since I met him, he has not only proven himself a master innovator in our industry, but, perhaps more importantly, a thought leader, pushing us gently and purposefully towards a higher standard of kindness, empathy and resilience. With Culinary Leverage, he lays bare not just his emotional personal history but a framework for living that applies equally to the pro kitchen, the boardroom, and the family table. His story will forever change the way I think about our food system and the extraordinary community of people who have dedicated their lives to the craft of cooking, at all costs.

—Gail Simmons, food expert, TV host and author of *Bringing It Home*

"Honest. Eye-opening. Harrowing. Brilliant. Douglas Keane's *Culinary Leverage* is a deeply grabbing look at the travails and high points of one of the world's best chefs. Anyone who thinks perfection comes easy, in any domain from food to law, business to music, should read this book. An homage to grittiness and sheer will, Douglas' story will stay with you for years."

—Neal Katyal, former acting solicitor general of the United States

"Yo, my man Douglas has a powerful story to tell and has proof of concept every night at his amazing restaurant Cyrus. Through his true honesty, passion and love- he is one of the best. Every industry could learn something about doing it better by reading *Culinary Leverage*."

—Randy Jackson, musician, television personality

"I love to work with clients that have big ideas and want to push boundaries, and Douglas Keane is exactly that kind of client. His vison for Cyrus 2.0 considered not only the guest experience, but the long-term happiness and success of his team, too. This book outlines an ethos rooted in care for food and for people that should be the new standard for fine dining."

—Tom Kundig, FAIA, RIBA, principal/owner and founder of Olson Kundig

"Just as he allows guests to wander his kitchen and even chat with the cooks, he has the unusual ability and willingness to let us inside his head as he negotiates life in what comes across as an almost impossible business in which to survive. No CEO whose organization I've written about—and that number is probably over 200--has ever offered more candor, frank talk, and self-analysis than Douglas Keane."

—James Heskett, UPS Foundation professor emeritus at the Harvard Business School

"A riveting and very brave book from one of my favorite chefs in the world. Douglas is a rare talent, deeply caring about his food and the way it is produced and procured and the impact of everything that happens from the fields, oceans, and farms to the final presentation to the guests. A must read in the annals of culinary storytelling."

—Chef Traci Des Jardins

Culinary Leverage:
A Journey Through the Heat
by Douglas Keane

© Copyright 2025 Douglas Keane

ISBN 979-8-88824-520-0

Cover photo by Jay Evan.

All rights reserved. No part of this publication may be reproduced, stored in a retrieval system, or transmitted in any form or by any means—electronic, mechanical, photocopy, recording, or any other—except for brief quotations in printed reviews, without the prior written permission of the author.

Published by

3705 Shore Drive
Virginia Beach, VA 23455
800-435-4811
www.koehlerbooks.com

Culinary Leverage

A Journey Through the Heat

DOUGLAS KEANE

VIRGINIA BEACH
CAPE CHARLES

This book is dedicated to the people in the hospitality industry who come home exhausted and wake up achy, sore, and tired but go back to work each day with a smile and a sincere desire to give their guests a beautiful escape for a few hours. You inspire me.

And to Roxie. The best of an incredible pack. You keep me going.

And to all the people with food "allergies," without you I might have finished this book a few years ago. You annoy me.

CONTENTS

Author's Note	1
Foreword	5
Chapter One	11
"Plush" (Acoustic) by Stone Temple Pilots	
Chapter Two	22
"Pink Houses" by John Mellencamp	
Chapter Three	27
"Watching the River Run" by Loggins and Messina	
Chapter Four	31
"The Lion Sleeps Tonight" by The Tokens	
Chapter Five	37
"Mona Lisas and Mad Hatters" (Live) by Indigo Girls	
Chapter Six	42
"Some Nights" by FUN	
Chapter Seven	48
"The Boxer" by Simon and Garfunkel	
Chapter Eight	53
"Maggie" by Frank Patterson	
Chapter Nine	56
"Round Here" by Counting Crows	
Chapter Ten	60
"On My Own" by Les Misérables Original London Cas	
Chapter Eleven	63
"I Can See Clearly Now" by Jimmy Cliff	

Chapter Twelve 68
   "Ho Hey" by The Lumineers
Chapter Thirteen 74
   "Time After Time" by Cyndi Lauper
Chapter Fourteen 79
   "Take A Chance on Me" by ABBA
Chapter Fifteen 88
   "Lola" by The Kinks
Chapter Sixteen 91
   "Sweet Home Alabama" by Lynyrd Skynyrd
Chapter Seventeen 95
   "Ironic" by Alanis Morissette
Chapter Eighteen 102
   "I'll Fly Away" performed by Gillian Welch and Alison Krauss
Chapter Nineteen 107
   "Landslide" (Acoustic) by Fleetwood Mac
Chapter Twenty 111
   "FourFiveSeconds" by Rihanna, Kanye West, and Paul McCartney
Chapter Twenty-One 116
   "Rockstar" by Nickelback
Chapter Twenty-Two 121
   "Royals" by Lourde
Chapter Twenty-Three 128
   "Back in Black" by AC/DC
Chapter Twenty-Four 136
   "In Your Eyes" by Jeffrey Gaines
Chapter Twenty-Five 141
   "Hook" by Blues Traveler
Chapter Twenty-Six 143
   "All For You" by Sister Hazel
Chapter Twenty-Seven 146
   "Superstition" by Stevie Wonder

Chapter Twenty-Eight 151
   "That Lonesome Road" (Live) by James Taylor
Chapter Twenty-Nine 155
   "Somewhere Over The Rainbow" by Israel Kamakawiwo'ole
Chapter Thirty 163
   "The Rocky Road to Dublin" by The Dubliners
Chapter Thirty-One 168
   "Lonely is the Night" by Billy Squier
Chapter Thirty-Two 175
   "She Talks to Angels" by The Black Crowes
Chapter Thirty-Three 183
   "Glycerine" (Acoustic) by Bush
Chapter Thirty-Four 193
   "Sympathy" by The Goo Goo Dolls
Chapter Thirty-Five 198
   "Old Man" (Live) by Neil Young
Chapter Thirty-Six 208
   "House of Gold" by Twenty One Pilots
Chapter Thirty-Seven 213
   "Waiting For My Real Life to Begin" by Colin Hay
Chapter Thirty-Eight 218
   "Hunger Strike" (25th Anniversary Mix) by Temple of the Dog
Recipes From the Heart 224
Acknowledgments 230
Photos 231

AUTHOR'S NOTE

I wrote this book because I want to make changes in the restaurant industry. I want to use my *culinary leverage* to push the hospitality industry into balance. It needs to take care of not only its guests, but its workers too. I was blessed to have parents who told me I could do anything. They encouraged me to work harder to do whatever I wanted to. And I did, sometimes to my body and mind's detriment. I fell deep down some rabbit holes and almost didn't come back up. I've learned over my thirty years plus in the industry while witnessing the imbedded dysfunction that *hard work* isn't enough on its own. Hard work and luck are *almost* enough to achieve success, but it takes reflection, mindfulness, and incessant questioning of the established norms to make serious changes. It takes standing up to bullies, and it also takes repeating over and over the phrase, "What if?" What if we thought about things just a little differently? What if we tried a different model? And what if we were the voice of change?

It's pretty simple, at least in my head. And due to circumstances, I've been seriously thinking about it for the last few years. With time brings clarity. Before the first Cyrus restaurant closed, I was in the thick of it and there wasn't even enough time to contemplate that the model was almost all wrong. It was *survive and try to thrive* mode at all costs. We seemed to care more about how or where our food is raised and caught versus how the people preparing it feed, clothe, and house themselves. We cared more about the number of stars clandestine critics (fronted by a tire company) awarded a chef instead of how the dishwasher could afford to buy tires for their car to get to work. And chefs cared more about getting those white-walled stars and how to innovate with the latest gadget or foam to create the next bite that would "blow your mind" than they did about innovating the staffing model and creating a stable environment for the team and the business. It stems from our obsession with everything *celebrity* in America, and how an industry founded on restoring people veered off course and headed full speed ahead into the cliffs of Covid that were always there instead of just popping up like we were misled to believe.

Challenging established norms and disrupting decades of dysfunction isn't as simple as my mind wants it to be. But if you trace the history of the hospitality business to its roots, it's about people taking care of other people. So, at its core the solution exists. Now we just need to agree that it's important and to take steps forward. We all saw what happened during Covid, and we all want our lives to be better. I have a few ideas that aren't just theoretical. I am living, breathing, and executing a new model at the improved Cyrus 2.0 in Geyserville, California. I have taken all my painful lessons, reflected on them, and put some ideas into practice. We are profitable and successful by any standard criteria, and we are also happy. We work hard and we all know we are part of something bigger. *A movement?* Maybe. *A catalyst?* I hope so. This is a first paradigm for the entire restaurant industry.

This book is my attempt to share what I think can help make a better environment for everyone—the workers, guests as well as investors. There are many more ideas to come, and I look forward to learning from the younger generation as they look at the current situation and implement even more progressive ideas. Even one simple revolutionary idea can spark so much change.

One invaluable idea is reducing staffing needs by 50 percent. Boom. I did. We all need a reboot and to start thinking a little more analytically. Example: let's say you have ten employees, and you pay them $50,000 a year, which is $500,000 in payroll. Cut it to five people and pay them $75,000. That's $375,000. What are you going to do with that $125,000 savings? First think about what those five retained employees are going to do with a 50 percent raise. It's life changing. No more debt! No more second job. Money to help retire. And most importantly they won't be looking at every job opening that pops up on their screen. They are going to stay with you much longer. Maybe forever, and if you're lucky become part of the family. That's a hundred and twenty-five grand that stays in your pocket. You don't need to sacrifice style or substance to achieve this; just look at things differently. Perhaps invest in technology to help one person do two or three tasks at the same time. Sous vide cooking, combination ovens. Things that can achieve perfection without a huge labor dedication. Invest in nicer tabletops—wood, granite, whatever you like. You don't need tablecloths, which can be expensive. You won't need a person to iron them or an extra staff member to change them during service. Instead of making ten different breads like I did at the first Cyrus, you can make two perfect ones and watch people enjoy them just as much. We used to give twenty different candies away at Cyrus 1.0. I paid two people to make and wrap candies because that's what you did at high-end restaurants. Then I asked a *what if* to myself. What if I could create something so spectacular that would end one's dining journey in a way they would never forget? An investment in a dream, but at the same time a reduction in labor. And the end result? Well, come check out The Chocolate Room at Cyrus. Style and substance, with a conscience.

Another reason I wrote this book was to show people it's important to stand up for your values. Yes, it's daunting, and yes it can be exhausting and sometimes expensive. The ugly truth is that there are people out there who will not only get in your way but will try to spite you just because of ego.

As you read my story you will see that I found my voice at pivotal times. I didn't back down to bullies. I took plenty of lumps and bruises along the way, but as Franklin D. Roosevelt said, "I ask you to judge me by the enemies I have made." I'm comfortable with my list. And as the character Rocky Balboa shared, "It's not about how hard you can hit; it's about how hard you can get hit and keep moving forward." Keep moving forward and throw a few punches back. Bullies are insecure, frightened people who need to be shown by example. A few names and places have been changed just to avoid any legal hassles. Some of the events and quotes described in the book are drawn from memory and may not be verbatim.

I have also been blessed with some incredible four-legged friends who have touched my heart deeper than anyone can ever know, and they are part of this story. They picked me up when I was so low that I couldn't imagine living another day. They showed me how to not give up and how to smile while struggling. They have taught me that unconditional love is real and worth striving for in all relationships. I wanted to memorialize their stories because theirs are so intertwined with mine.

Writing this book has been cathartic, a cleansing. And if by doing that I can help even just one person escape their darkest saddest days then it will have been worth it. I'm overdue for some sort of confession. I want to apologize for unknowingly hurting people, and for taking part in an industry that has hurt its own for so long. I'm not just reciting that here. I am putting it into practice with an amazing team of people who believe we can make a difference while still trying to obtain the elusive perfection that fine dining can provide.

Style and substance with a conscience and connection.

I hope you enjoy my adventures in *Culinary Leverage*.

Douglas Keane

FOREWORD

I probably should have read the manuscript before agreeing to write a foreword to this book. Somehow or other, I assumed it would be about food and the ingenious business plan Douglas Keane and his team put together to create and present some of the finest gourmet cooking anyone could hope to enjoy. After all, I had just completed a case study on Cyrus, their restaurant, for use in teaching principles of service management at the Harvard Business School where I was a faculty member for many years. It wasn't as if I was totally unfamiliar with Keane's cooking and Nick Peyton's hospitality, having experienced them fifteen years apart in both Cyrus' 1.0 and 2.0 versions. But I had assumed that the book mainly would be about the tastes that Keane honors and savors in his cooking. I had no reason to believe that it might also include the taste of a gun barrel in his mouth.

There were two reasons I agreed to do this sight unseen. First, I bet on the guy. I'm not always right, but I've been lucky that way. This was someone who is passionate about what he does. More importantly, he's passionate about the people he's doing it with in a business in which that is not always the case. I was quite certain that would come through in his writing. And he was passionate about getting the case study of Cyrus written. I've rarely experienced the kind of cooperation—emails returned in five minutes early in the morning after a night of entertaining (not just cooking for) guests at Cyrus—that Douglas provided during our case writing experience. He was so personable and approachable that it was easy to forget that the entrepreneur I was dealing with was a rock star in his field; internationally known; the recipient of Michelin Stars; winner of the James Beard California Award for culinary excellence; winner of the *Top Chef Masters* contest on television. It was unthinkable that he might have battled depression.

The second reason I agreed is that I have the kind of interest in food engendered in someone who, having never cooked in his life, was forced into four years of cooking for the final four years of the life of his Parkinson's afflicted spouse. While I didn't always see it that way then, I see it now as a love offering to a lifelong partner. Sure, I had tried to get out of the job of cooking for my spouse and her caregiver by bringing in prepared food or hiring a caterer. But both of them said they preferred the taste and freshness of my cooking more. So four years in the kitchen it was. Nothing fancy, but something tasty and nutritious. Living alone, I suppose I should go out more. I prefer my own cooking. Of course, upon reading the manuscript, I found that Douglas Keane had gone through much the same experience with his father.

I'm not a foodie. After all, I grew up on a farm in Iowa where the three-meat dinner was a feature of haymaking and threshing seasons. If my family didn't offer ham, chicken, and beef (like everyone else), they were running the risk of not getting a full crew of volunteering neighbors back the next year. The three-meat dinner was consumed at noon after a morning of haymaking or threshing in ninety-five-degree heat and ninety-degree humidity, and before a thirty-minute nap out on the lawn in the shade before the return to the fields for an afternoon of even more intense heat and humidity.

But I had watched my grandmother prepare the best apple pie I've ever tasted, my mother smear the cream cheese on the crust of my favorite birthday strawberry pie, and my partner prepare the best pie crust anyone could ever make, using just barely enough water to hold the pastry together while ensuring that it would melt in your mouth when baked. I didn't realize that I had always preferred being with the women in the kitchen rather than with the men in the living room. But as I write this it's coming into focus. On the eat-to-live/live-to-eat scale, I tend toward the right. Douglas Keane has helped me realize that.

Douglas offers us in this book a unique combination of extensive knowledge about what he terms a *broken* process for preparing and presenting gourmet food along with a very human business model for repairing it. He loves people as much as he loves food. (Don't ask him where dogs rank in his heart.)

The book is about an ingenious business model, carefully crafted by Douglas and Nick Peyton during an enforced ten-year recess from the fine dining business. It illustrates so many service business principles that an entire course could be taught about it. Among other things, there is the notion of the *cycle of excellence*, the belief that if you design bigger jobs, hire fewer people who are willing to both learn and teach, pay them well, provide liberal benefits including paid vacations, and celebrate their work, you can actually save money by reducing team member turnover and the productivity loss that goes with it as well as recruiting, hiring, and training costs. It's about first delivering an outstanding team-member experience so team members can deliver an outstanding service experience to guests, what those of us who teach service management call "the mirror effect." It's about hiring for attitude, then training for skills—not the other way around. It's about the notion that everyone learns—and teaches.

It's about a guest experience that is unique in the business, one that is delivered in a special setting that emulates one's home. There are separate and ample spaces for enjoying a pre-dinner drink along with some canapés, early-course dishes in the kitchen, more formal dining in the dining room, and a room for a final treat near the exit. The beautifully equipped facility combined with ingenious cooking routines both minimize labor and make heroes and heroines of the staff, all of whom are *on stage* (to use a Disney term) during the evening. It's a symphony in which everything and everyone are in tune.

Douglas, Peyton, and their crew even perfectly get the service bookends—the first and last impression of the evening's journey—

right. The five basic flavors of the five canapés at the beginning are matched by the five basic flavors of the chocolate truffles at the end.

None of this is possible unless the business model delivers revenue and cash to the bottom line. So we put what we have called over the years the "service profit chain" to work: team member engagement and loyalty leads to guest satisfaction and loyalty that in turn produces growing revenue and profit. Bingo!

There is much more going on here that applies far outside the fine dining business. Of major importance is the process by which the business plan for Cyrus 2.0 was put together in the first place. It's based on three questions: What do we hate most about this business and its management traditions—leadership by fear, over-the-top behaviors, the noise, the hours, the burnout, the low pay? Why have we put up with these for so long? How do we get rid of them en masse?

Attention must be paid to the team-member experience. But there isn't any team-member experience without guests. How are they typically served in a gourmet restaurant? Does everyone enjoy sitting in one spot through a three-hour-tasting experience? Is that how we entertain at home? Of course not. Why not try to emulate that kind of experience that we enjoy so much, one in which we spend the evening in different parts of the house among a small group of friends that's not too difficult to cook for, a group that can fit around our dining room table?

The planning process illustrated here is a work of craft worthy of emulation in other businesses.

None of this works without the food and the chef. The imagination on top of the basic knowledge of food and tastes that Douglas Keane brings to the table is displayed in a continuing parade of ingenious dishes that make up the twenty course Cyrus dining experience. This is experimentation and creativity in the context of a lot of food science that commands a great deal of respect, as much as for a great jazz musician.

The real story is about how Douglas grew his knowledge and developed his skills to the point where he could achieve these things. Just as he allows guests to wander his kitchen and even chat with the cooks, he has the unusual ability and willingness to let us inside his head as he negotiates life in what comes across as an almost impossible business in which to survive. No CEO whose organization I've written about—and that number is probably over 200—has ever offered more candor, frank talk, and self-analysis than Douglas Keane.

You'll know why I agreed to write this foreword without having read the manuscript after you've read this compelling book.

James Heskett
UPS Foundation Professor of Business Logistics, Emeritus
Harvard Business School
Sarasota, Florida

CHAPTER ONE

"Plush" (Acoustic) by Stone Temple Pilots

Restaurants, as a whole, are notorious for being bad investments. So, a potential investor needs to see a very compelling package to be motivated to place their trust in a restaurant owner to shepherd their hard-earned money. It's a lot to ask. Still, many people over the years offered to invest in Cyrus 2.0. They loved our history and new concept. More importantly, they had faith in us. But since we had had the partnership with a single investor funding us over the previous five years, we had politely declined. When that partnership ended, my business partner, Nick Peyton, and I had to dust off our old rolodex and go out and find backers—something I truly dreaded because I know full well that I'm not good at it. And that was before this thing called Covid came along and dismantled the industry overnight.

To be clear. Covid alone did not cause all of the problems in the restaurant industry. The industry is ripe with dysfunction; low pay, long hours, mistreatment of employees, a lack of healthcare, and low profits are just a handful of issues. The pandemic was simply the straw that broke the camel's back. The quarantine that began on March 16, 2020, brought to national and international attention the ills of the restaurant industry. Restaurants survive day to day and week to week, not quarter to quarter. With no cash coming in, huge amounts of payroll to pay, and no end in sight, many restaurants had to shut their doors permanently. The one good thing about Covid for restaurant owners and workers was that it brought awareness to the systemic issues the industry faces, giving us a chance to make some progress.

Nick and I picked ourselves up, began the search for a new location, and started all over again. It was frustrating, daunting, and invigorating all at the same time. We soon found the perfect location that was unique, modern, secluded, and perched above the vines. Though out in the countryside, which we desperately wanted, it was easily accessible. The building had sat empty for the last fifteen years since its modern makeover from an old prune packing plant in Geyserville in beautiful Sonoma County. A few people had looked at it over those years but couldn't make sense of what to do with it. It was a big space with zero street presence, technically a horrible location for anything that required onsite customers. But that type of location and footprint were exactly what we wanted. Our concept of moving people around called for more space than a typical restaurant that serves thirty-six to fifty people a night. And engaging a guest to turn onto a long driveway and hear the crunch of gravel under their tires as they approach a beautifully lit, modern, glass and stone building perched over the vineyards, would transport them to the beginning of a magical evening.

On February 8, 2020, we signed and secured the thirty-year lease with a right of first refusal to purchase the property and were having great fortune raising money for the project. Every time we were able to get a potential investor to meet with us to walk through our vision at the building and grounds, we got a commitment to invest – many sent checks immediately. At the time, we anticipated that we would need six to eight million dollars to open. We obtained commitments of six-and-a-half million and had over two million in hand. In just one month, we were on track to close out our offering within the next thirty to forty-five days.

What could go wrong?

On Sunday, March 8, 2020, after an introduction by another investor, Nick and I gave a tour to a very nice husband and wife with a very wealthy family name. This particular family with three children could not stay long, as they had soccer games back in San Francisco to attend. So, we put our usual tour into overdrive to accommodate their schedule, and after fifteen minutes, we had a handshake for $200,000 for two units committed. The husband asked me to call him in a week to finalize.

At that point, Nick and I didn't know if we needed to keep going. We knew from past experience that a few people might flake before they cut a check, but the response had been so overwhelmingly great that we were positive we could easily fill those potential voids.

Again, what could go wrong?

On March 16, 2020, California announced that it would effectively be shutting down. The order to shelter in place was delivered. The world ceased all travel. Hospitals filled up. It didn't really register with me at that time how widespread Covid was. I understood that it was significant, but I thought it would only be a problem for a month or so, at worst.

I was supposed to call the San Francisco couple back to secure their investment. But I also knew it was an awkward time to call. I figured I'd wait a week or two for things to settle down and give him a call. I remained confident. We had the coolest building, location, and concept, and we weren't going to be ready to open for at least twelve to sixteen months. So, I believed that Covid wouldn't affect us much. As we all know now, those early weeks of Covid thrust the world into a black hole of sorts. The pandemic didn't settle down, and we had very little control over our lives.

On March 26, I reached out to our San Francisco investor.

"Yeah . . . hey man," he said in the kind of tone used to convey condolences after the passing of a loved one. "We've been thinking of you guys this week."

I knew in that instant that he wasn't going to wire the money.

"Listen," he said, "we're going to keep our powder dry for a while and see what our friends need and not make any investments at the moment. If this clears up, please check back in with us. We'd love to be a part of what you're creating."

I was pissed. But not at him. I got it. It made complete sense. Even though they had oodles and oodles of money (think Rockefeller-type money), I couldn't blame him. In the previous seventy-two hours, all restaurants had been ordered to shut down, and there was no end in sight to the pandemic. And he wasn't the only investor who had committed but not yet paid. There were several. I began to feel the entire project slipping away and a crippling fear that I wouldn't be able to pay back the investors who had already provided the funds we spent on lawyers, architects, and permits. Despite the fact that this entire scenario was unprecedented, I couldn't bear the thought of letting those investors down when they had placed their trust in me.

A familiar sinking feeling overcame me, the same forlornness I had felt after a beloved dog passed away, the one I felt when I was forced to close a very successful restaurant years earlier, and the one I felt the night I drove drunk because of an identity crisis and almost killed myself. (I'm forever grateful that I didn't hurt anyone else in the process). I never really recovered from those events; I just kind of pushed on.

This time, the feeling was darker. I didn't know how fragile I was at the time, but I did know I was walking a psychological tightrope.

Despite the ordered shutdown, I was still being held to my lease requirement to get a land use permit for the location. Even if I could have obtained logoed HAZMAT suits, I still wouldn't have been able to get anyone to see the space in person. Still, I had to keep going as if Covid presented no obstacles.

Nick and I hired two companies to make videos for us to help sell the investment, in the hopes that we could somehow continue the work through the pandemic. If we couldn't get potential investors to come see the space, then we would bring the space to potential investors. The two videos were incredible and energized our fundraising efforts. It was slow moving, but it was all we had, and it gave us hope.

Casting a wide net is fundraising 101. However, it's easier and safer when you have some sort of connection to a potential investor. Before Covid, we were getting introductions to friends of friends of friends with very little connecting thread. But since the pandemic, the investing environment had changed as more people were spending more time connecting online—a place where deception is easily achieved. For those of you without experience in the field, you should know that when you are raising money and getting pinched, you tend to want to believe people who tell you that they are going to give you money. And, if you get a recommendation about a potential investor from someone you know and trust, you'll likely take that potential investor at their word.

There were a few rules that I wish someone had told me: The first is that the people who tell you how rich they are up front are lying. If, in the first two minutes of the conversation, they brag about their net worth, their huge house, or their $200,000 car, they're full of shit. The second rule is that people who tell you that they will take the entire investment (or the entire remaining portion) in the first phone call are 100 percent full of crap. Third, the person who sits quietly, asks good questions, and makes no grand promises is the keeper.

I could fill up a few chapters on how I fell prey to people in first two categories. In two separate instances, a con artist from Vancouver, Canada, and a MAGA prick from Michigan each promised large amounts of money. In the end, I was played for free dinners to the tune of tens of thousands of dollars. The introductions to these two thieves came from people I believed were friends, but these friends turned out to be as complicit as the cons themselves.

This took a toll on me.

I had to write a brutal email to all of our investors letting them know we had been played—*twice*. Humiliation doesn't adequately describe the feeling. *Am I this stupid?* I asked myself. *Yeah, it sure seems like I am.* I sat down and wrote, in a nutshell, *I'm sorry. I'm an idiot. You trusted me with your hard-earned money, and I blew it. And I'm out of time. I'm sorry.*

Hitting send on that email to the investors broke me.

I could taste salty, sour, and warm. No sweet, a little bitter, but no umami for sure. The bullets were in the clip and loaded. I wanted to see if I could do it. *I'm ready*, I thought. I didn't know how to pull myself out. I'd conjured a thousand different scenarios as to how to survive my impending failure, but the brutal truth was that I didn't want to survive. I could not face this magnitude of failure. My reputation would never recover. I couldn't handle the thought any longer. Still, I took a moment to review the day in my mind.

When I'd woken the next morning, it was clear that this would be the day that I died. But first, I called a close friend who I had recently grown very close to. I wanted her to know why I made that choice to kill myself. I also thought she would have a good perspective from which she could help my family, friends, and coworkers process it all afterward because she was privy to my history and struggles in a way that they weren't. I didn't have a game plan when I called. I just told her what had happened. I know my voice was soft and quiet. I know she could sense my pain. Five minutes into the call, I started to feel guilty. Confessing my intentions to kill myself wasn't fair to her. It was a self-centered move. So, I simply let her know how much I appreciated our friendship and that I was fine. Then, I told her I needed to go.

I was surprised by how warm the barrel felt in my mouth and by the tangy taste of the steel. I've got a very sensitive gag reflex, and the barrel activated it. I'd need to relax to prevent throwing up. I really didn't want vomit all over my lap in addition to making a mess of brains splattered on the wall. Then the thought suddenly occurred to me that it would bother me if people thought I was scared. I wasn't. I just wanted out. I breathed a little bit to relax my throat. *I can do this.*

I thought about my friend Colleen from Green Dog Rescue who chose to end her life. I was pissed at her for leaving us, but I also understood that she made that decision for herself, and it was her right, however sad. Same with Anthony Bourdain. Sometimes, you just want out. I was there. I was numb, I was defeated, and I just wanted out. No more failure, no more setbacks, no more rejection, no more con artists from Canada and asshole MAGA Republicans from Michigan. No more telling investors I fucked up and was going to lose their money. No more avoiding my wife, Lael, so she couldn't tell how close I was to calling it quits.

I thought back to my last appointment with my shrink who asked if I was suicidal. I bald-faced lied, which seemed like the only power I had left in this world. All of my culinary leverage felt like it was spent, and what little I had left was taken away by Covid and scam artists. If I'd told my shrink or my marriage counselor of my suicidal intent, they would have had to report it. I would have lost the power to choose for myself. I wanted that power to end my life.

And yet, as logical as my thought process seemed to me at the time, I never pulled the trigger. My finger went to it a couple times, and I felt at peace and in control. I could have pulled it, and that's what I needed to know at that moment. Knowing that I *could* was enough to break the spell and consider what would happen if I had. Roxie, my beloved chocolate Labrador McNabb pit bull mix, was on the other side of my bedroom door. I could hear her pacing. She would not have understood. And I imagined Lael coming home to find the mess in our bedroom. I mean, she'd have to get a new bed for sure. *Damn*, I thought, *I don't want her to be the one to find me.* That wouldn't have been fair to her.

I reconsidered. If I was going to do this, then I'd do it outside in a place that's easy to clean up, and definitely not at home. *But where?*

I locked the gun back up in its box but kept it loaded. Then, I took it to my office and hid it behind my desk for safekeeping while I devised a less messy plan. I thought about my upcoming fiftieth birthday the following month. Why not make it to that miserable milestone and then pull the plug? That would give me time to button stuff up a little better to protect Lael from any fallout and to help wind down the business, so it didn't all land on Nick. That made sense to me. It was like I was giving myself one more chance. I also needed to consider my exit a bit longer. Depression had numbed me to caring about making it work, and yet I was somehow still in pain. It's such a hard state to describe. I hurt . . . *bad* . . . *really bad*; but I also couldn't feel anything. I was spent.

Later that day, a friend asked me to help him move some stuff across the country. The thought of driving through Middle America where no one would know what an utter failure I was seemed like a good way to pass a little time until my birthday. I could still work on tying up the business and getting affairs in order for Lael on the road. Initially, I fantasized about simply going off on my own during the trip and just disappearing. Let some random sheriff in a random town find me. Less mess at home. And even if it ended up a few days before my birthday at the time, as long as I completed the work for Nick and Lael, that seemed to be a solid option.

In preparation for the journey, I set off to say goodbye to some people in a way that wouldn't give away my plan but that would give me a chance to tell them that they were important to me. I also wanted to somehow communicate that my decision was not because of them. They would have hospitalized me had I told them of my plan.

After my goodbyes, I ventured cross country with my old pal. Though there were many opportunities in which I could have ended it on that trip, I didn't. We traveled through eight different states all the way to the East Coast, parted ways in Nashville, and I flew back for one more stop in Southern California before heading home to Sonoma. When I reached my last destination in Manhattan Beach, I walked the beach alone.

At some point on that walk, the thought occurred to me that I should reach out to one of our early investors, Scott Marlette, who lived near Manhattan Beach. Scott had been an original investor and had held on through all of the drama. In the moment, I just thought about him as a person—not a business partner—he was a good one. He never criticized or complained, and he had remained a steadfast supporter of Cyrus. I just wanted to convey my gratitude.

Scott and his wife, Stephanie Schaffer, had no connection to Nick or me or Cyrus besides dining at the first one in Healdsburg. They invested one share because a friend of theirs suggested they might enjoy being a part of this. The friend, an original investor, referred to Scott as a keeper. I mainly dealt with Scott during the process. He was polite, inquisitive in a professional way, and showed great enthusiasm for the restaurant and our new way of thinking about the business model. When I asked for the check, he replied, "I'm not going to wire until you raise all the money. I'm not going anywhere, I promise. I just do not want to waste $100,000 if you can't get there. But I reiterate: I'm not going anywhere. You can take as long as you need." *Fair enough*, I thought. He would occasionally check in to see how things were going and offer any help he could.

We met for breakfast and just chatted. He had already gotten the letter about the con artists, but he asked about what I did after and what I planned to do moving forward. I didn't realize it then, but I was being interviewed. And I guess my brutal honesty got me the job, so to speak. I had about four weeks left before the project would be officially over. If I didn't have the money to start and finish construction in four weeks, then it wasn't happening. I said this to him with zero expectations. Really. To me, at the time, it was just breakfast between colleagues.

I left the meeting thinking that I was glad that I had had the opportunity to meet with Scott. I sincerely liked him as a person. Perhaps it was just enough of a positive experience to shift my brain chemistry the fraction necessary to make me consider not pulling the trigger. Maybe it was something else altogether. I honestly don't know what made me hold off on executing my plan on that trip. *I can do it later*, I assured myself.

When I arrived in my hometown, I went to my office first to check in on the gun. My cell phone rang; it was Scott. *Huh, curious*, I thought.

"Hey Douglas," he said, his tone upbeat. "Stephanie and I really believe in this concept and in the staffing model and especially in you and Nick. We want to support your vision and make sure it comes to fruition. We'd like to take the rest of the investment and get construction started."

There are people who want you to succeed. There are people who pay it forward. There are people like Stephanie and Scott and many of our investors who believe in something and are willing to put their hard-earned resources toward it. I try and be grateful for these people every day.

Yeah, they are keepers.

And just like that, I didn't have time to plan where I would shoot myself. I had a restaurant to build. Clarity to keep trying came to me in an instant—to connect with people and get the help you need when you need it. I knew I had to call a doctor, and I did. I knew I needed to surround myself with good friends who could support me, and I did. I knew I needed to get outside and walk with my dogs more, and I did. I got the help I needed, and I also got lucky. If you find yourself in a similar mindset to what I experienced during this dark time, don't wait for luck to convince you to get help. I shared this because I want you to know that you can get through a time like this, too. There are people in solid organizations who want to help you, and they're just a phone call away at the Suicide and Crisis Hotline. Dial 988. These trained professionals care, and they provide free and confidential support. If you're afraid to make that phone call alone, there is a friend out there who will dial that number with you. Please just ask.

For some of us, our mental health might be a life-long battle, but that doesn't mean we can't get healthier and experience more good days than bad with a little help. I have many friends who fight this good fight daily. I believe that the current state of the restaurant industry is toxic and acts like a petri dish to grow depression, anxiety, and despair. That's why I set out to change it—to create a healthier, more peaceful, and more joyful work environment. The chapters that follow tell the story of how I grew to love cooking starting at a very young age and eventually developed a new way of working in the restaurant business.

Today, Cyrus, my dream restaurant, has a unique staffing model that allows us to support one another in living a healthier work-life balance. We're thriving. It's now clearer than ever to me: I had all the *culinary leverage* I needed all along; it's serving others so we can be healthier together. You have this power, too, in your own circles. I hope that reading my story gives you a little inspiration to serve others and yourself in the process.

CHAPTER TWO

"Pink Houses"
by John Mellencamp

Dearborn, Michigan, where I grew up, was not without its flaws. Its ugly racial history still ran deep when I was young. At times, Dearborn presented an atmosphere of intolerance that was hard to navigate as a kid growing into an adult. But I'm thankful for that perspective; and even today, it helps me to better understand some of the current political climate. My greatest professional and personal assets including my palate, my intense work ethic, and my relationship with my extraordinary mentor, Stan Bromley, originated in that imperfect town.

Mom was the cook in our Dearborn house. Never tiring, she would work a full day at her own business, a salon called Foxy Lady, and then come home and cook dinner as Dad watched a game. I never understood why it was her job to cook. She worked just as much as Dad. It bothered me that he didn't help her, but it didn't seem to bother her. Back then, in the late 1970's to the early 1980's, society seemed to say to women who worked that they better have their homes in order, too. I'm so thankful that Mom taught me through her actions that a strong, independent woman deserves respect. Mom's example had a lasting effect on my success as a chef. But that desire to help Mom out in the kitchen when no one else did was the spark that ignited the beginning of my culinary education.

Mom was a great cook, and I'm so grateful for her culinary talent.

She exposed me to all kinds of food as a child. She knew acid and seasoning, and she had a great sense of taste, referred to in the culinary world as a *refined palate*. She was focused, organized, and precise in her kitchen. In her blue-denim apron with a smiling pig wearing a chef's hat, she taught me how to toast walnuts for chocolate chip cookies as James Taylor played through the stereo in the background. No pre-bought chopped walnuts for Kathy Keane's friends and family. Nope. We toasted whole walnuts in the oven until we could just smell the aroma. Then, we patiently allowed the toasted walnuts to cool before grinding them in the small, hand-crank mill with the white plastic top and clear glass bottom. I learned quickly; too fast and the walnuts would almost puree; too slow and the mill would clog.

To Jimi Hendrix's "Purple Haze," Mom taught me how to toast peppercorns in a sauté pan before grinding to bring out as much flavor as possible in her legendary Cajun shrimp. She taught me to squeeze fresh lemon juice instead of using the pre-squeezed, pasteurized crap in the little plastic lemons that every other Midwest mother used. I also learned to appreciate the importance of fresh citrus zest and room temperature cream cheese when making blueberry cheesecake to the smooth sounds of Loggins and Messina. Mom's understanding of food and seasoning undoubtedly helped me to refine my own palate over time—a necessity to a good chef.

I've often stated that I could fix a lot of bad food with salt and lemon juice. Seasoning, at its simplest definition, is just salt. It's the amount of salt needed to flavor an individual piece of food appropriately. A piece of salmon cooked perfectly, but without any seasoning (salt), has almost no flavor. It's not worth the calories. Add the right amount of salt, and you have something beautiful to share with people. Some chefs throw pepper in with salt as seasoning. I don't. Pepper is a spice to be used when you want that flavor, just like when you use cinnamon or clove. Not using salt is *never* an option. I'm not a doctor or a trainer. I make dinner.

The second most important part of creating something flavorful and pleasant to eat is balancing the acid to make the item exciting and to give the palate relief from the fatigue of a one-dimensional taste. Take our perfectly cooked, perfectly seasoned piece of salmon from above. Then, add some freshly squeezed lemon juice. Boom. Balancing seasoning and acid will fix almost every meal you could ever want to make. I hope I didn't just put my consulting business in the red, but the thought of all of you readers missing these simple steps and the tastes that come from them bothers me. Salt and lemon juice, people. Some cooks have a natural instinct about how to create this balance in their dishes, and others learn it with guidance. Mom was a natural. From an early age, I could taste the difference between her food and other moms' food. The other kids' moms would work just as hard and cook beautiful meals, but the flavor was often lacking. I was appreciative of their efforts, but I always wondered why there was such a difference. Years later, I realized that my mom understood seasoning and acid, so everything she made boasted lots of flavor.

A strong work ethic is just as important to the making of a good chef as a refined palate. It would have been impossible growing up in Noel and Kathy Keane's house at 6 Fairmount Court in Dearborn, Michigan, to *not* adopt an intense work ethic. Grade school and high school were too easy for me. I wasn't challenged at all by the academics. Plus, the high value of exhausting physical labor grinded into my psyche by my parents seemed more rewarding than the potential benefits of cerebral work. I loved digging ditches, mowing acres of grass, and even working the honey wagon with my best friend, Mario, and my brother, Chris, at my father's side business—our campground, Robin Hood of Sherwood Forest. Yeah, it was a stupid name; Noel wasn't the creative one. I learned to crave actions that yielded immediate gratification. I fondly recall Sunday afternoons after Mass spent at Mom's salon scrubbing the cigarette smell out of the ashtrays and bleaching perm solution off the floor, while DJ Casey Kasem played Joan Jett's, "I love rock n' roll" in the background. That was rewarding. Memorizing the Gettysburg Address in Mister Antczak's eighth grade social studies class at Divine Child Elementary School was not. The praise from Mom and Dad coupled with the visible accomplishment of hard, physical work, formed an addictive foundation for my work ethic. Here I am, all these years later, still doin' the same fuckin' thing—exhausting myself with physical work and seeking praise. My willingness to work hard for those affirmations has been my spinach, but also my kryptonite. Maybe I should've studied harder.

As mentioned, my mentor extraordinaire was Stan Bromley. Stan is known in the hospitality world as The Butler to the Stars and Dean of the Hotel World. We aren't bonded by birth or by blood. But Stan has and will always be an important part of my family. Stan and his wife, Julia, entered my family scene shortly after their arrival in Dearborn for Stan's new role as the general manager of the then soon-to-be newly opened Hyatt Regency, a huge landmark for the city and the first stunning modern building Dearborn had seen. It was Henry Ford's vanity project.

The Bromleys and the Keanes all became fast friends. Dearborn had an odd new couple in Stan and my dad, Noel. Stan's wife, Julia, and my mom were two peas in a pod in that they both had endless energy and interests, extremely kind hearts, and deep intellect.

My first memorable interaction with Stan happened on a two-car dual family road trip to Ranch Rudolph when I was five years old. I'm told that back then, in 1976, I was remarkably cute, a little needy, and highly talkative.

Just before leaving, the then childless Stan cheerfully offered, "I'll take Dougie."

In my youngest child mind, I imagined that my mom, dad and older, perfect brother, Chris, all silently and joyfully nodding to each other as if they had just won a Return to Having One Child lottery, an early 1970's version of The Hunger Games. They devilishly knew what Stan was blindly walking into when he voluntarily swapped Julia out for me.

I don't remember what I talked about on that ride. I *do* remember that about ninety minutes into the drive, Stan pulled over on the highway. Such a drastic measure was usually reserved for a flat tire, puking passengers, or other road trip emergencies. My parents quickly scrambled halfway in between two idling cars to meet Stan.

"He hasn't stopped talking since we left," Stan blurted. "Take him back, *now*."

Although our first road trip together might not have been deemed a successful bonding experience by normal standards, something happened in those ninety minutes that solidified *Doug the Rug* and *Stan the Man's* forever bond. A lifelong friendship without normal borders or the confines of traditional labels was born. My relationship with Stan progressed from that of a crazy uncle and spoiled nephew to mentor-mentee, to best friends, and to a second father-son relationship. There hasn't been a significant life event, and many insignificant ones, that Stan hasn't been a part of.

Everyone loved Stan. I realized early on that I sure wasn't going to follow in my father's footsteps and become a lawyer; that course was obviously charted for my school-loving older brother. And I really had no desire to run a beauty salon. But I liked cooking with Mom, and I liked Stan. I tested the cooking flame my mother kindled by enrolling in culinary classes with Sister Josephine at school. It was there that I realized that I was a natural at it. I liked it. I also got a prom date. But most importantly, I realized during that time that it made people happy when I provided them with food, and that made me happy.

Stan got me a job bussing tables at the Hyatt Regency's restaurant, and I found the energy addictive. As I leaned in closer to Stan and his foodie world, our friendship evolved into a professional one. With sincerity, my personal Yoda had been inadvertently grooming this young culinary Skywalker. Over the next decade, Stan would guide me to apply to hotel school, connect me with the right interviews for the perfect jobs in New York, and help me to navigate a path in the bumpy restaurant world with a calm assuredness. There are so many gifted chefs who didn't have a Stan—someone to talk to and to bounce ideas off of, and someone who cares about them completely and unconditionally. I'm guessing Tony Bourdain and Bernard Loiseau didn't. Stan could have run after the Ranch Rudolph car ride, and I'm lucky he didn't.

CHAPTER THREE

"Watching the River Run" by Loggins and Messina

On a crisp fall evening during my sophomore year of high school, my parents took me to look at Labrador puppies. It was a surprising outing as there hadn't been much talk about it. I suspect that my folks were thinking that our dachshund, Dolly, who was currently thirteen to my sixteen years old, was not long for the world. My brother, Chris, was off at college, and my folks wanted insulation and distraction for me when Dolly checked out. Looking back, this incident illuminated the fact that my parents didn't know me that well. I was somewhat conflicted about getting another pup, as I was pretty loyal to Dolly. She was my sister. I vividly remember the moment she popped out of the box one Christmas morning. Dolly was technically meant for my mom, but Dolly and I had found each other that morning and rarely left each other's side thereafter. Still, I knew I had room in my heart for more than one, and, after some introspection, the thought of raising a puppy seemed like the gift of a lifetime.

The forty-five-minute drive in my dad's spacious, black Lincoln Continental took us to the steps of a nice big suburban house in Royal Oak. As I stepped inside, I felt like Charlie entering Willy Wonka's Chocolate Factory. Fuzzy little white and golden fur balls scurried with boundless energy in a penned part of the kitchen. I said hello to the proud momma Labrador as I sat on the floor to meet her offspring. The first one, a chubby little boy, climbed right up on me. Unbeknownst to me, my parents had already decided we were getting a girl. When they lifted up the little guy's tail to check his equipment, they immediately dismissed him. The poor pup slunk away with visible sadness. He had heard them and somehow understood. It broke my heart.

But then, just like that, *she* jumped in my lap. Sweet to no end, she locked her puppy eyes on me with a wagging tail.

"Okay," my dad said. "That's the one. She picked him."

I saw Mom roll her eyes. My dad's epic impatience was kicking in again. This was the guy who would leave before the encore song at a concert and before the last out of the baseball game so he wouldn't get stuck in traffic. My mom's expression conveyed that he had just taken all of the fun out of picking a puppy. But that time, Dad was right. She did pick me. There was no need to keep looking. That was my first experience with a connection that organic. It just felt right.

On the drive home, my new puppy, Maxie, had a visceral realization. The effusive joy she had found with her new best friend subsided as she realized that she was in a strange place with people she really didn't know. The little fuzzy brothers, sisters, and mom she had known since birth ten weeks earlier were nowhere to be found. She lurched up to the back window and started to cry for her family. I teared up, too. I got it. How scary. Quietly, I resolved that she would never be alone.

"I got you, little girl," I promised.

That night, my parents decided that Maxie should sleep downstairs in the basement, in the furnace room, by herself. *Hmm*, I thought. Even as a teen, my perception of this suggestion was that of ripping a ten-week-old baby girl away from her family and then isolating her in a dark, damp, scary basement setting. *Am I really related to these people?* I wondered.

"Let's give her your jacket so she can smell you and not be afraid," my parents suggested.

Oh, yeah. We've known each other for about two hours, and the scent off my cold jacket will really comfort her. For two successful and intelligent people, I still to this day can't fathom their reasoning. About seventeen minutes after my folks finally went to sleep, I traipsed off with a pillow and blanket and headed down to the basement for my first of many slumber parties with Maxie. I remember thinking that I could live down there with her.

Even before Maxie, I had a deep-rooted affection for all animals. I felt for them in an innate way. I could understand them. We trusted each other instinctively, and we enjoyed each other. My family and friends have tried to pinpoint and even psychoanalyze where my strong bond with animals originated. If it's karma or justice-based, then my bond with animals came to be because my paternal grandfather, Joseph Keane, was such an abusive, alcoholic dick that I have spent my life making up for the atrocities he inflicted on the stray dogs of Dearborn as well as for the trauma he inflicted on my dad and on his siblings.

Joseph Keane, on his weekly stumble home from his local on Friday night, grabbed canines off the street and dragged them home to perform the sadistic act of cropping tails down in the basement as his five children watched in horror. Yeah, it's that awful. If I'm repenting for his sins, then so be it. Or maybe my love for animals evolved because I wasn't super close with my mom and dad as a kid. I always felt like kind of an outsider compared to my perfect older brother. Dolly and Maxie were my closest friends, my comfort, and my support. Maybe I don't like people that much because I've been let down too many times by their flaws. Animals, on the other hand, are incapable of deceit or ulterior motives. Animals are naturally honest and love unconditionally. I believe that animals deserve our undying loyalty for their contribution towards making this world a better place. For that reason, every major decision I've ever made, including college, jobs, relationships, and housing, has taken into consideration my bond with them.

This life choice to make the animals in my life a priority has brought challenges. My allergies became unbearable almost immediately after we adopted Maxie. There is nothing quite like the shedding of a yellow lab. Think of an Everlasting Gobstopper, but with fur. The doctor informed my parents that my allergies were so severe that we would need to get rid of all animals in order for me to breathe well and prevent the development of asthma. *Yeah,* I thought, *that's not happening.* I had made a promise to Maxie in the backseat of that Lincoln. I would deal with a runny nose and some Albuterol.

A few years later, our veterinarian informed us that Maxie had the worst hip dysplasia he had ever seen and stated that we should put her down immediately. I walked out of his office sobbing. But the minute I got home, I called the veterinary school at Michigan State University, which was just starting to do hip replacement surgeries on dogs. I got my girl fixed up in no time. It's a good thing, too. Without Maxie, there's no way I'd be where I am today.

CHAPTER FOUR

"The Lion Sleeps Tonight" by The Tokens

"You got in!" she screamed over the phone. My mom's voice cracked with audible tears of joy and amazement.

I didn't expect to get into Cornell University. I was extremely excited about the possibility of attending Florida International University (FIU)—beaches, women, sun, and ocean. Maxie and I would love it. I hated the Michigan weather from my first snowbound steps. It just never clicked with me. There is nothing pleasant whatsoever about numbing feet and hands and sniffling noses upon the first inhale of Arctic air. It took twenty minutes to scrape off my windshield on many days. Why live like that if you don't have to? I was ready for the beach after eighteen years of weather misery.

The festivities of my senior year spring break trip to Fort Lauderdale were supposed to be interrupted by a side trip to FIU in Miami. I was going to take the bus down, tour the campus, meet a few faculty, and then promptly return to the debauchery back in Fort Lauderdale with Mario and the rest of the Divine Child Hooligans—Bill Terski, Joe Vetting, Mark Starosciak, and Matt Throm. The lads of our blessed crew had all convinced their parents that an unchaperoned vacation with the goal of perfecting underage drinking while attempting to contract multiple STDs was an important rite of passage.

But the call home to check in two days before my planned side jaunt changed a few things. Mom had opened my mail and was barely able to contain herself. My parents hadn't expected me to accomplish much. I wasn't the serious one. I wasn't a natural athlete. Sure, I worked hard. But I wasn't Ivy League material.

"It must be a mistake . . . a computer error," Mom's Tourette's slipped. I found that funny at the time—I mean, kind of. At that point, my perception was that the most impressive benefit of the acceptance letter was that it cancelled my need to leave Fort Lauderdale and interrupt the party. That was a good enough reason for me to celebrate. I hung up and went to join my high school mates to share the good news. Maxie and I were both going to Ithaca in upstate New York—or so I thought.

Maxie and I had been inseparable through high school. The soft, blue fabric material in my Ford Ranger pickup was constantly matted with white-yellow hair on the passenger side. I made friends ride in the bed of the truck if Maxie wanted to go, which was always. When I prepped for SAT and ACT tests, I promised to figure out a way to bring Maxie with me to college. As sure as I was that I wanted to follow my mentor Stan's footsteps into the hospitality world by attending a hotel school, I also knew that I needed my animal anchor to function. Unfortunately, I couldn't keep my promise to Maxie, and my first days at Cornell were miserable. The place was beautiful, the weather was damn near perfect, which would be short lived. My dorm room at 301 North Baker Hall was straight out of a picture book. Ivy climbed up the old, grey stone walls, and gorgeous trees with fall-stained colors danced in the warm winds rolling off Cayuga Lake. But I wasn't ready to be away from home. The hardest pill to swallow by far was that dogs weren't allowed in the dorms. What the fuck? Who was I supposed to talk to? I needed Maxie.

When my brother left for the University of Michigan, my father pulled him aside and advised him to loosen up and have a few beers.

Noel's parting words for me were slightly different: "Dougie, all you need is a 2.0 to graduate."

My flannel shirts and baseball caps seemed a little out of place at Cornell. Everyone seemed smarter than me. I wasn't really sure why I was there. I felt like a Great Lakes fish jumping into the Atlantic. The other students weren't bad kids, they had different upbringings and different values. It seemed like years of prep school palaver drilled into their ethos created a sense of entitlement. For many of my classmates, Cornell was their destiny. To me and a handful of others, we were starry-eyed and dewy-like. I'd like to personally thank Colonel Frank Slade from *Scent of a Woman* for those last few lines.

Even with the fish-out-of-water feeling and stage-four homesickness, this was the best thing that could have ever happened to me at that point in my eighteen-year-old life. It would be the first of many situations for me that cemented my belief that taking young people way out of their comfort zones and forcing them to challenge their habits and beliefs is vital to defining who they really are. I didn't want to become entitled like a lot of my classmates. In fact, entitlement is my least favorite human trait, as it breeds laziness and hatred. But being around those students for four years enriched my life in that I found myself and defined my core values. And even though most of the students were not my cup of tea, I found my small pack, people like my roommate of all four years, Paul Epstein, who, to this day, I cherish. And Carlos Silva-Craig, who I accidentally sat next to in Hospitality 101. And on the first day we both broke into uncontrollable juvenile giggles when the name of the woman sitting right next to us was called and had the word *balls* in it. Yeah, we realized we were sharing one brain between the two of us. And a few others you're about to read a little more about, including Robbie Dawe, Tony, and OJ.

The schoolwork was as challenging as the social climate. I struggled to keep focused and motivated. My heart was set on learning to cook, and I couldn't see how the classwork was going to help me. In the back of my mind, my father's 2.0 comment played on a continuous loop. In addition, during freshmen orientation weekend, the president of Cornell, Frank Rhodes, had given an inspiring speech about the amazing things Cornell had to offer. Mr. Rhodes had finished with a line that I decided to take to heart: "Don't let the schoolwork get in the way of your education."

Thus, I was drawn to the kitchens, and the classroom seemed like a time-consuming detour. My parents, who had anticipated that I might struggle academically, asked me to not get a job my freshmen year. They generously promised to take care of any and all incidental needs. They just wanted me to focus on studying; no job and no dog.

The no job thing lasted a few months. I couldn't help myself. I walked into Johnny's Big Red Bar and Grill with one of my roommates, Nick Weaver, as he was looking to bartend. The manager of the bar, a six-three tall man with a chiseled frame that conveyed a discipline as solid as his no-nonsense attitude, looked right past Nick, annoyed by the audacity of a mere freshman asking to bartend.

"What about you?" the manager, Tony Kalyk, asked looking straight at me.

"I can cook," I responded nervously. I really couldn't cook for a bar and grill menu at that point, but he didn't need to know that. Besides, I knew I'd figure it out.

"Okay, you're hired. Come back tomorrow."

That was the beginning of a life-long friendship with Tony that I still value to this day.

Working gave me a sense of structure. It was real and tangible as opposed to the heady and hypothetical classroom lessons. I didn't want to make waffle fries and Johnny burgers the rest of my life; I had higher aspirations. But I did enjoy the heat, the sweat, and the exhaustion at the end of the shift. It allowed my brain to slow down just enough to jump into the books.

But life at Cornell still wasn't working quite right. So, my second year, I returned to Cornell with my blue pickup and my blond girl Maxie in the passenger seat. I found an apartment that allowed dogs;

life was good. With her new hip, she was ready to take on the Ivy League and give me a hand, too.

Every year, as classes got a little more intense and demanded that extra level of attention, I could feel my lack of interest in academics compound. It's not that all of the classes were painful or uninteresting; I just failed to see the practical connection to my chosen field. We were in the business of cooking, cleaning, and serving. How could anyone be good at that or lead other people to do those tasks without at least mastering them first?

I was surviving Cornell with Maxie and my job working in a kitchen. I was also lucky enough to be mentored by a few professors and instructors like Dr. Chris Mueller, Chef Bob White, Chef Brian Halloran, and Giuseppe Pezzotti. Those men took a liking to my blunt opinions and Midwest work ethic and went the extra miles for me.

When I returned to Dearborn from my summer job cooking in San Francisco just before my third year started, a letter from Cornell was waiting for me. It was from Dean Michael Redlin, whom I had never met. Just for context, The Hotel School at Cornell has around eight hundred and fifty undergraduate students, like a small high school. Yet Dean Redlin and I had never had the pleasure of each other's company.

"Your obvious inability to compete with your peers . . ." was the highlight of the two-paragraph billet doux.

It seems my previous semester's grades had dipped a little below the dean's liking. As I didn't fail any class and got credit for everything I took, I chuckled that my just getting by must have really pissed the dean off. "Dean meet Keane." The words of my father's inspiring college sendoff replayed many times as I digested the letter. I felt a little bit of embarrassment mingled with a lot of rage. I mean, the guy really could have called and asked me what was up, investing maybe five minutes of time. But nope. *Thanks, pal.*

That letter sparked two important decisions for me. First, I resolved that there was no way in hell that I would leave before my degree was delivered to me by the prick who wrote that letter. I persevered through sheer determination. Maxie and I graduated in 1993, four years after I entered the fluorescent-lit rooms of Statler Hall. No extra time was needed. I kept that letter close by, determined that there would be an appropriate time to revisit it. That letter had fueled my tenacity and would do so again during some of the harder times in my career journey. Perhaps I should thank the dean for that.

In 2010, seventeen years after I had received the disgraceful letter from Dean Redlin, I stood in the wings of the Hotel School auditorium at Cornell, preparing to take the stage and speak at an event with Chef Bob White. Chef White was one of the cherished few who had mentored, counseled, and befriended me during my college days. I credit him as being instrumental to my graduation. He pulled me aside right as I was being introduced to the crowd of four hundred students, faculty, and industry VIP's. He let me know that he was proud of me, and he chuckled as he mentioned that I almost didn't make it.

"Yeah, we had some doubters," I offered back in bond.

As he grabbed me and offered a fatherly hug, I teared up and asked him to make sure he at least listened to my intro and the first few minutes of my talk. He assured me that he wouldn't miss a second.

The master of ceremonies introduced me as the only Hotel School graduate to ever achieve a Best Chef James Beard Award, Two Michelin Stars, and a Four-Star Review. I had been waiting for that moment for almost twenty years. I walked to the podium, and with a shit-eating grin, I thanked the master of ceremonies for the lovely intro. I even referenced a few of the awards. Then, I pulled the letter out of my coat pocket, smiled at the audience, and asked them to indulge me for a minute as I read a love letter from an old friend who had declined my invitation to the event.

CHAPTER FIVE

"Mona Lisas and Mad Hatters" (Live) by Indigo Girls

There was something comforting about the grittiness of New York City after Cornell. It was loud and intense, but it was also real. The polished skyscrapers on Park Avenue, glistening in midday sun, were stunning and intimidating in their own right. But juxtaposed next to the scurrying pedestrians and hot dog carts billowing scented steam into the air, those symbols of success somehow seemed within reach.

In the culinary world of 1993, no city in the United States could hold a candle to New York. The entire food world was centered around the happenings of its chefs. San Francisco, a very distant second, was barely on the radar, minus a few notable exceptions. The raw and abundantly forged ingredients of intensity, money, and pressure made a recipe that bred excellence, perfection, and ego—if you could last. I knew this about Manhattan. I had watched *NYPD Blue*. So, I was ready.

In addition to my formidable *NYPD Blue* education, my mentors Chef White, Chef Halloran, and Stan had primed me to put my head down, work my ass off, get yelled at, and become a cook. Although there had been a brief moment of consideration in regard to attending culinary school, I easily dismissed that option as the thought of any more time in any school setting made me want to buckwheat myself ala *Things to Do in Denver When You're Dead*. Plus, there was a girl in New York. The work route was an easy choice.

I scored a job at The Four Seasons, one of the busiest, oldest, and most famous restaurants in Manhattan. They shouldn't have hired me, but they did. The only thing I had going for me was my connection with my Cornell faculty advisor, Professor Tom Kelly, who had a long relationship with Alex and Julian, the owners of The Four Seasons. I also wanted the job bad.

The first few weeks were a little brutal for this bright-eyed Midwestern kid. The Big Apple took a few bites out of me. I had to leave Maxie in Michigan until I could figure out how strict the pet policies were in available apartments. Then, I left my wallet in the back of a cab one day. Another day, the girl I had been dating for more than two years decided to introduce me to her new lover by *accidentally* inviting me over to walk in on them. It was my first human heartbreak, but good lessons about human trust and character flaws were the silver lining. Plus, she was only studying to be a doctor. It would have been a big loss if she had been in veterinary school. That experience refocused me on just learning how to cook. I would be able to wall off those types of relationships and just keep it very casual for a while. It was New York City, after all. But the beginning of my time in New York left me with no cash, no ID, no dog, and no girl.

"DUGLESS WHAT THE FUCK ARE YOU DOING, YOU STUPID FUCKING ASSHOLE?" Chef Christian Albin, called Hitsch, could be intimidating as hell with his huge bellowing voice and his deep, Austrian accent. He was strong, short, and stout with a thick, dark brown 1970s style moustache. He screamed orders into a microphone, commanding his loyal army of cooks who were scattered throughout a kitchen the size of half a football field. Sure, we were technically getting yelled at. But with Hitsch, there was a jocular tone to his yelling. He was performing for us in a way. His crassness and bullying were just part of the show. If Hitsch was running a kitchen this way today, his ass would be sued up and down 'til Tuesday. But back then, the unified goal was to produce great food as fast as possible and keep the machine moving. Hitsch was our conductor, and he was brilliant at it.

The Four Seasons was intense. Fast lunch. Fast dinner. Great ingredients. At that point in my culinary journey, it was the most complicated food I had ever seen. We would do two hundred lunches, slow down and prep for a few hours, and then go right into five hundred dinners. My head was spinning from the second I clocked in each day. I was confident I was going to get fired at any point. They would have had every right. I was slow.

"FASTER DUGLESS, FASTER DUGLESS . . . FUUUUUCK!" Hitsch belted out over the PA system in between lines of "Don't Cry for me Argentina." He would always get a laugh.

After a few months of pure fear and being out of my league, everything in New York started to click for me. I finally got Maxie moved into my 74th and York third-floor studio, and the tasks I needed to master in order to become the chef I wanted to be became clear. My neighbor and new best friend, Rochelle, helped me with Maxie while I worked twelve-hour days, and I felt pretty content that I was right where I needed to be.

Speed was critical. Everything moved fast in New York, especially the kitchens. But the speed had to be controlled with precise movements made with clear purpose. The ability to taste and think quickly were key. Everything had to be tasted in each step of the process in order to know how to adjust seasoning. My stomach had to be ready for an enormous amount of calories each shift, yet I still never felt satiated due to the lack of a proper meal. I had to master repetition, the ability to do the same task over and over all night and not get bored. To be a great line cook, you need to cook something hundreds of times with the exact same attention on the two hundredth attempt as you had on the twenty first.

It was intoxicating to survive on that line in those times. In our Grill Room lunch every day, leaders of industry that I read about in the *New York Times* enjoyed the food I had helped prepare. Anna Wintour, Henry Kissinger, Martha Stewart, Jackie Kennedy, and Philip Johnson came to The Four Seasons for the quality and the reputation that I had become a part of. At dinner time in the Pool Room, more of the New York City elite, celebrities, and tons of people going to see Broadway shows came to experience a meal that only The Four Seasons could provide.

"PICKUUUP . . . four Dover sole, six racks of lamb, three veal Four Seasons, and two duck . . . PICKUUUP!" Hitsch barked into the microphone, his mouth covering the fuzzy ball on the top.

"YES CHEF!" we answered as we scurried to assemble his order. We always hoped and prayed that he wouldn't pelt us with the next order before we could finish the first. But it never worked out like that.

The noise was intense, but the heat created its own energy. It was unrelenting. Dinner alone was five hours of nonstop moving and twisting, lifting plates down to the boards on the pass, plating, and saucing, then pushing them out to the waiters. The fear of messing up someone's dinner or not being able to keep up with everyone else fed our stress levels and fueled our speed and endurance.

A common conversation I had with Maxie while sipping a twenty-four-ounce Budweiser can out of a brown paper bag during our stroll at the end of each night went something like this: *"But you're so close to the top of the ladder, Douglas. You're at one of the best restaurants in the best food city in America. Just stay afloat. Keep your head down. Keep working hard. It won't be that hard in a few more months. You might not walk in terrified one day."*

I was learning so much. Not only could I handle a sauté pan and move quickly, but I could make stocks and sauces. I started to learn how to butcher. The lifers in the kitchen thought I was crazy because I offered to do their work if they would show me how to do it. Some of the guys had more than twenty years of experience at their stations. Oscar made the crab cakes. Guy-O grilled massive, perfectly cooked steaks. Sammy was the fish butcher, and Lanza was the saucier. Patrick was the master pastry chef. These guys were pros, and I was actually getting paid to work with them. I had found my place in the world, and I was slowly getting better at cooking each day.

At some point, I think that everyone at The Four Seasons realized that I was their project. I was the youngest kid in the kitchen by far. We all knew that I was going to move off at some point to go learn from other kitchens. But while I was there, they made sure that their little brother was a sponge. I don't know why I fit in so well with that group, but I'm forever grateful for their efforts.

I walked home most nights from the side kitchen entrance 52nd and Lexington to 74th and York, where I lived. This became a twenty- or thirty-minute motivation session in which I absorbed the lessons of the day. This small-town, Midwest kid craved the energy circulating in Manhattan close to the midnight hour. The smells of New York City aren't always pleasant, but alive in my mind forever will be the fresh scent in the air after a late evening rain in the summer. It was like the city just emerged out of a pool accompanied by a soothing, warm wind. As I walked towards the East River, I savored the fact that I'd survived another day in one of the best restaurants in the best food city in America. This was exactly what I was looking for. I was tired, proud, and making people happy. It was then that cemented that cooking was my vocation.

CHAPTER SIX

"Some Nights" by FUN

The amount of pure culinary talent in New York was intoxicating. As my skill level increased, so did my appetite to learn. I was well positioned to take advantage of the wealth of knowledge within a short subway ride in any direction. A *stagiaire* (stah-gee-air), or in kitchen shorthand, a *stage* (stahg), is a French term that defines the tradition of cooks spending time observing at other restaurants. Cooks have a relentless need to check out what is happening in other restaurant kitchens. Our curiosity compels us to find out what they are cooking and how their lines differ from ours. Being a stagiaire is also a great way to find your next job. With the current labor laws, it's practically illegal to stage now; the cook has to sign many unenforceable waivers and ridiculously paranoid nondisclosure agreements. But back during my time in New York, when I met another cook at a bar, my first question was always, "Where do you work?" This question was followed immediately by, "Where have you staged?"

I spent many of my days off staging at different restaurants, always excitedly nervous to see what they would allow me to do when I got there. I could spend my day picking parsley for eight hours, which was fine as long as I kept my eyes wide open to observe. But if I was really lucky, I'd get to jump on the line and cook a little. I was happy just to be there.

I had decided to leave Four Seasons to spread my wings a little. I was getting too comfortable there and starting to envision staying there indefinitely. Even though it felt like family in that kitchen, I knew that I was too young to set down roots. I had places to go and chefs to learn from. I needed to get pushed into more uncomfortable situations to keep growing. So, I ventured out and decided to take some time and pick the right spot. I staged and ate out as much as I could to find the right place to sharpen my knives next.

One of my best friends from Cornell, OJ, was working in the kitchen at a place called Picholine on the Upper West Side. We worked hard, partied hard, and discovered that girls liked cooks for some reason. I'm guessing Maxie's presence helped attract a few young ladies that would normally not have given me a second look. I'm not that proud, so I'm okay with that. As for OJ's charm? Well, he was with me.

We had eaten at Picholine once and had been blown away by the food. It wasn't mind blowing in the sense that I couldn't understand it. Rather, the food was perfectly executed with details a few steps above what I had been cooking. I was really intrigued. The chef was Terrance Brennan, a fine Irish name I thought, and he was damn good.

OJ and I pretty much drank together every night after work in any bar that would allow dogs, swapping stories about what we had learned that day and dreaming up what we would cook when it was our turn to be in charge. He invited me to come stage at Picholine.

I had already staged for a few days as they didn't have a job available at that time. I was more than happy to hang out and work for free. I was into day four when the butcher unexpectedly quit—a no show—a cheap and spineless move. Please cooks, give your two weeks. If they throw you out, at least you can hold your head high. So, the butcher was gone, and one of my weakest skills was butchery. I wanted desperately to get better. So, I offered my services for free. I would do the job for two weeks so I could practice while they found a real full-time butcher.

I started the following morning at seven cleaning black sea bass and racks of lamb. After I finished, I would go upstairs and jump on the line for a few hours to help. I loved the food, and it was refreshing to be in this high-powered New York kitchen.

A few days into the stage, Brennan offered me a job. *Never let good talent get away.* Terrance had pulled me aside and said something had opened up. *No shit,* I thought. Two people had no-showed that day, but Brennan showed no visible signs of panic with his staffing shortage predicament. Instead, his demeanor seemed to say that all was good in his kitchen.

I could continue my butcher stage for the next ten days (yeah, the free one), and I could then come up to the hot line and actually get paid. The offer was five hundred a week.

I did some math in my head and replied, "Chef, I would love too, but I don't think I can pay rent and health insurance on that. Can you come up to six hundred a week?"

I wasn't trying to be cute or to leverage him. Literally, I just wanted to be able to cover my essentials. Food could come out of my small savings. I was on a mission to learn a craft, and this was the only way to go about it—scrape by, make ends meet, and good things would come later.

Terrance looked back at me and replied, "Sorry; I can't afford that. Five hundred it is."

I took a deep breath. "Chef, can I think about it for the night? I really need to figure out if I can live on that. I'll still do the butchery for free for the next two weeks no matter what if you want."

"Sure," he replied, extending his hand with a kind of smile. I shook his hand, and we wished each other a good night.

I showed up the next morning and butchered as promised. I waited until after lunch was over, and I had finished all of the meat and fish.

"Chef, can you sit? I have thought about your offer."

"Yeah, of course," he replied.

"I'm sorry, Chef, but as much as I really love this place and your food, I can't afford to take the job." I felt bad for saying no as I wanted to be there, but I couldn't risk the lack of health insurance. "But I'm happy to keep butchering for the next ten days like I promised."

"WE HAD A FUCKING DEAL. WE SHOOK HANDS!" he screamed across the table as he pounded his fist and rattled his espresso cup, which spilled out onto the white, starched tablecloth.

At that point, I wasn't sure if he was more pissed at me or that he had to change a tablecloth. Either way, it was obviously all my fault. I decided then that I was being accused of breaking a deal. I tried to defend my honor by reminding him that we shook hands good night and that I was going to *consider* if I could take his offer. But I have heard that when bulls see red, they lose the ability to reason. Instead of having a discussion like a normal person, he huffed and he puffed and he knocked his espresso over.

"GET THE FUCK OUT OF MY RESTAURANT, YOU PIECE OF SHIT!"

The volume of this rapid-fire edict was matched by the red bursting from this angry Irishman's face. It happened so quickly in our otherwise calm conversation that, for a quick second, I thought he was joking. No fucking way we went from a quiet discussion about a reasonable counteroffer of $100 more per week more than what he had offered me the night before to screaming like this. Just no fucking way.

I think my smile pissed him off more. I wasn't trying to irk him, but the absurdity of his outburst just made me realize how much this guy, this celebrated chef, had lost it. Sure, Hitsch screamed, but he screamed for Dover sole and rack of lamb. In my opinion, Brennan seemed unhinged, and I felt pretty sure he wanted to hurt me. So, I instinctively smiled. I know, I know, why would I smile? It just appeared, the only physical representation of my nervousness and amazement. I had heard all of the stories about screaming, violent, New York City chefs. But this seemed almost like a caricature of itself; only it wasn't. So, I smiled. And as I smiled, I was mentally fast forwarding to how I would tell OJ later that night at the Raccoon Lodge how this Looney Tunes had lost his shit.

Yep, with that scream and my spontaneous smile, it was on, just like Pamplona. I headed towards the kitchen to gather my knives; I'd left them by OJ's sauté station. I returned OJ's bewildered look with an expression that communicated that he'd be paying for beers later. The bull's horns were closing in on me. The unfortunate detour into the kitchen had cost me some valuable escape time, and the odds of getting gored had increased.

Mere inches from me as I walked out of the kitchen and down the narrow corridor to the exit, Brennan screamed down my back, "YOU WILL BE FORTY-FUCKING-YEARS-OLD AND NEVER KNOW HOW TO COOK A FUCKING THING."

Hmm, I thought. *I heard something similar back at Cornell. I wonder if Terrance and Dean Redlin hang out?* I thought he wanted me to hit him, but I had zero desire. I was having fun watching him melt down. I was hoping he would hit me; it would have been fun to beat him in his own restaurant. But I also knew that half the kitchen would have run out to his aid. He was the cult leader; even OJ would have been torn. I know that my laughter at that point was the red flag waving in front of the bull, but I couldn't help it.

OJ paid for beers that night. By the way, completely unrelated to my running of the kitchen bulls, OJ was culturally forced to switch his moniker back to his birth name of Oliver a few months later after the famous white Ford Bronco chase. Look it up, millennials. It was special. You can literally trace your Kardashian roots right back to that moment. Type in "OJ Bronco Kardashian." Do it. But that night, OJ, not Oliver, and I laughed a lot and processed that bizarre episode while I drank for free and OJ introduced me to the bartender each round as his "thirsty, twenty-four-year-old friend who still won't be able to cook when he's forty." This was one of many nights that formed my resolve to treat my future employees well.

In 2009, fourteen years later and just two years shy of the Nostradamus of kitchens prediction, I won the James Beard Award for Best Chef of California. Terrance, whom I hadn't seen since the day he kicked me out of his kitchen, and Oliver, who I spoke with almost daily, were both coincidentally in attendance. I had two Michelin Stars and four *San Francisco Chronicle* stars. Terrance didn't. I had written part of my acceptance speech with a special thanks to the angry Irishman who threw me out of his kitchen and told me I would be forty and still not know how to cook a thing. I had wanted to end that speech with my best Al Pacino's Colonel Frank Slade impersonation and state, "Fuck you too, Terrance." For several reasons, Lael talked me out of that ending. She said that it was beneath me, and I'm supposedly not that petty.

Hey Terrance, thanks for buying the book, pal.

CHAPTER SEVEN

"The Boxer"
by Simon and Garfunkel

I've learned that my epic impatience can be both my spinach and my kryptonite. I get shit done. In the restaurant business, that's a necessity. It's also advisable to sometimes slow down and look at things from all sides in civilian life. Maybe sometimes in restaurants too, but I'm a slow learner. In my quest to keep learning my craft and simultaneously start a career, I had often created conflict by making quick decisions and going for it despite Stan's warnings.

"No fucking way," Stan said when I told him I wanted to take a job at Lucy's in New York City. "It's not a good idea. Just stay put and keep learning."

I'm still not sure why I took the job at Lucy's. The money was better than what I was making, but that wasn't it; a big paycheck was never the point in my young career. The food wasn't what I wanted to cook either; it really had no soul at all. I guess I just needed a break from a high intensity kitchen, and I wanted to test my wings as a chef.

In our daily phone calls, Stan kept telling me that I'd hate it there, not learn anything, and be stuck for at least a year. I decided not to listen to him.

Lucy was high energy, loud, and in your face. But she was also very sweet to me. I liked her. The energy she exuded was intoxicating and a little exhausting. This restaurant was not about the food. It was about Lucy and the uber-rich Upper East Side guys who frequented Lucy's—a private club in a way, but not exactly. I was just supposed to make the food. I was the only cook/chef in the place, a one-man show, and it was kind of fun. It was really a nightclub with gorgeous waitresses, bartenders, and guests. Oh, and it had some food.

I put my head down and worked hard for her for a few months. I made a little cash and had some fun via Lucy's excursions out into the New York City nightlife with her wealthy and beautiful friends. She liked to drag me out with them. I don't think she quite understood me that well. I was the super serious guy from Detroit who worked twelve-hour days and took care of his dog. This wasn't my scene. But looking back, maybe I was drawn to it to push myself out of my comfort zone.

Stan was right. I wasn't challenged at Lucy's after the first two weeks. I had it figured out, and I wasn't learning a thing. But I had committed and wasn't going to bail on her. Plus, the girls were hot.

One particularly rough service night at Lucy's after I cleaned up the kitchen and was ready to head out, I stopped to say good night to the boss lady. Lucy was taking in the chaos unfolding in her establishment. Upper East Side guys loosened their ties and bought expensive bottles of champagne for gorgeous young women while two girls were making out on top of a table. It was a little surreal. I was tired and wondering why I hadn't listened to Stan.

Lucy's deep, rough, heavy eastern European accent juxtaposed perfectly against her slim, white complexion and her jet-black hair that matched her black leather pants. Think, Joan Jett's mom. In a creepy familiarity, her voice was not unlike my Swiss-Austrian friend Hitsch's, who used to bellow my name back at The Four Seasons.

"DUGLESS, what's wrong?" she questioned, obviously sensing my discomfort with the debauchery on full display on the table where my spaghetti had just been eaten—or not. I was definitely the first honest cook she had who wasn't going to fuck her over and leave. And my food tasted good.

"Is it too crazy for you?" she asked.

Not wanting to offend her and also fully realizing that I had signed up for this, I shrugged the comment off. "I'm glad you are busy, Lucy," I replied. I knew how hard she worked, and I wanted her to succeed. "I'll figure out how to make it work for me."

She was always quick to take the conversation to the gutter at any point in the day. I liked her for that. It made it easy to break the ice and keep the long days light and inappropriate. Our banter in 1996 at Lucy's wouldn't fly in today's PC environs. She once asked me if I knew how to eat pussy the right way, in the middle of the day in front of the cute bartender, Anna. And if I didn't, she offered to teach me. *I'm not in Kansas anymore,* I thought. I blushed and answered that I was fine in that category, but if need be, I would reach back out for guidance. I found it funny, actually. Until that point, I had only known men as sexual harassment instigators. I thought I could take it to try to balance the scales a bit. Plus, she was trying to be funny, and I never felt threatened.

But on this evening at her bar, I focused my eyes on a stunning woman. She was supermodel-like, really. She was five foot eight and in shape. Her skin glowed, and her dark-blonde hair glistened. Her face was intoxicating, and I couldn't help but stare. I obviously said something to Lucy along the lines of "holy shit" or "wow."

"You like that, DUGLESS?" Lucy graveled back at me.

"Yes, Lucy," I answered in a way that conveyed my annoyance and implied, *Who the fuck wouldn't?*

"Do you want her, DUGLESS?"

"Um, yeah Lucy."

I had no intention of talking to that gorgeous woman. She was a guest; I was a cook. I was sweaty and tired, and I'm pretty sure she must have smelled like orange and honey blossoms. She was out of my league, and I was happy to just ogle her for a second.

"I'm going to get her for you," Lucy offered into the open world.

I laughed, not really understanding her.

"She's fifteen hundred a night, but I will treat you. You deserve it, DUGLESS."

It did take a second for me to understand what Lucy was saying, but I got the meaning . . . after all, I was Ivy League, you know.

That was the moment the lightbulb *finally* went off in my head: the eleven out of ten scale women with the little, rich white guys; the endless parade of money, coke, and high-end booze; the crazy table dancing and the girls making out in front of the entire dining room; the food that didn't really matter; the paycheck; and the hours Lucy spent in her office with the doors locked. It was just possible that Lucy's wasn't a restaurant or nightclub after all. Was it a place for rich guys to hang out and rent gorgeous women? And was I cooking food for them? Yeah, it was possible, but I never found out.

On a Monday morning not long after my illumination, there was a call for me at the bar. I never got calls at work. I don't know if I ever gave the number to anyone. It was weird. Dr. Ringold, "Rocky, or just Rock," was about as close a family friend as the Keanes had. He had known my mom and dad for many years. He was our doctor, our friend, and a business associate of my dad's. He was embedded and invested in everything Keane. But he had never called me.

"Doug, its Rock. I'm going into surgery right now, but I needed to call you. Your dad is very sick. We just got him out of an MRI, and he has a bunch of tumors in his brain. We're sending him to the University of Michigan Cancer Hospital, right now."

I didn't know what to say. I could smell the chicken stock cooking in the kitchen. It was time for the stock to come off the stove, and I needed to tend to it. But I couldn't speak. Lucy was close by. I don't know if she could read my body language and was genuinely concerned for me, or if she was just being nosy, but her presence at that time made me uneasy.

I knew what Rocky was telling me, but I couldn't grasp what it meant. There was a deep internal struggle happening in real time inside my head. It's not what you think, by the way. The struggle was that I couldn't figure out how I could get home to see my sick father. I was Lucy's only cook. She relied on me. We were open six days, and I worked every service. There was no one to fill in. Likewise my brother

Chris and I were the only ones who could be there for him back in Michigan. He had previously destroyed his marriage to mom upon deciding to screw a woman a year older than my brother who he eventually needed to get a restraining order against.

I was literally frozen in thought and in loyalty. *My dad or my boss?* Noel Keane, the lawyer, would have understood the dilemma. He caused it. I needed Rocky to say it.

"Rock, how bad is this?" I managed to utter.

"Doug, you need to come home right away."

"Okay, Doc. Thanks."

I hung up, looked at Lucy, and told her that I needed to go home ASAP. She knew I wasn't going to screw her over, and she knew how important this was. She offered to help me book a flight. I would take the redeye home on Saturday, see my father, and then fly back on the Sunday redeye to get to work on Monday by dinner. It made sense to me. It was the only option as far as we all saw it. *Let that fucking sink in.* My dad was dying. He was about four hours away by flight, and I couldn't figure out how to get to him until five days after the call. And I would only be home for twelve hours before I had to cook dinner for rich white guys that I didn't know, who really only cared about securing the hottest piece of ass they could afford for the night.

That's possibly the most disturbing part of the hospitality industry—the confinement. People who spend their days at work taking care of others can't even remotely take care of themselves or their loved ones. The industry runs on razor-thin profit margins in most cases and pays workers very little. The onus falls on the employee to show up, or the machine can't work. Think of handcuffs (but not golden by any means) that only come off at night for sleeping and maybe drinking, but that then get shackled right back on the next morning. Birthdays? Don't even ask. Weddings? No way. Weddings are on weekends. Hospitality industry workers *always* work weekends. Vacations—seriously? *Please.* Funerals? Only if it's close family—extended family be damned.

And for what? Why do we do it?

CHAPTER EIGHT

"Maggie"
by Frank Patterson

After six months of caring for my dad, I found myself at the cemetery on a brutally cold February day. Detroit is famous for them. Once you step outside and breathe, your nostrils flair, and it's almost impossible to catch a deep breath. I left the Lincoln, Dad's Lincoln, running so Maxie could stay warm. It didn't seem right to have her outside. The workers made quick work of the hole. The backhoe operator was skilled. They hoisted his box near the fresh grave and rested it next to the large, harshly angled opening. It seemed odd that I could smell the dirt in that extreme cold, but it came through. It seemed like an almost clean scent in contrast to the biting wind that had been pelting me since I stepped out of the warm, black car and told Maxie, "I got this girl."

They handed me a shovel. *Fuck. This is really it.* I wasn't ready to let him go. I missed waking up at three in the morning to make sure he didn't need anything. I missed putting a damp cloth on his head to cool him down from his sweats. I wanted to wheel him out to his car one more time and take him for a ride, pour him a glass of merlot, and make him mashed potatoes and steak, anything to keep him longer. I'd choose prime New York strip, center cut, generously seasoned, and seared hard in a cast iron pan that crackled when the steak hit the just smoking oil. A good two or three minutes on each side would develop a beautiful crust. Then, into the oven for just a few minutes before returning it to the stovetop. Add a hunk of butter, smashed garlic clove (skin on), and a sprig of thyme. With a good soup spoon circulating the butter and oil at a constant pace, the butter would emulsify and form a beautiful foam that perfectly butter bastes the meat. Dad loved how that looked and smelled with the garlic lightly toasted in the slightly browned butter. The entire kitchen would carry that aroma for a few hours after, and we both loved it. I'd finish his mashed potatoes while the steak rested to medium, super buttery and piping hot. A big dollop on the plate, maybe two, and then the sliced steak, but not too thin. He'd smile and look satisfied as he took a sip of Markham merlot. It was the greatest reward just to see him happy and not in pain. The ability to alleviate his ails and burdens with a simple meal cooked with love is a memory as seared into me as the crust he loved was seared onto his steak.

I gave the supervisor a nod to proceed. He had been pleasant and helpful, if somewhat misunderstanding of my deep need to see this to the end. A few hours earlier, just after the priest's final prayer in the warm cemetery building, I had realized that my job wasn't finished; I needed to watch the placement of his coffin into the ground. The supervisor had suggested that wasn't something I wanted to watch. *Fuck you, pal. He's my dad, and I'm not leaving him alone.* I would see him to the ground. As the mourners bombarded our house, *his* house, I grabbed Maxie and a bottle of Jameson, and I bolted. (Sorry, Chris. I needed to be with Dad one last time.)

It had been six months since Maxie and I had left Lucy's and New York to take care of Dad. It was my 'round-the-clock job I shared with my brother, Chris, and it was the best thing I'd ever done in my life. It was a time filled with countless medicine concoctions and injections, awkward showers, runs to the ER, a priest saying last rites a couple of times, and chicken salad sandwiches with extra mayo when he could still eat. I did my job well, and I was finally able to give him a fraction of something back for all he had done for me. I did it with pleasure and the goal of trying to help him keep some of his dignity while he died.

To pack up and leave New York City and move back home to take care of him wasn't a hard decision. Once I took it all in after flying on the redeye and back six months earlier, there really wasn't any internal debate about it. It was just happening. The work was physically and emotionally exhausting, and it was the toughest six months of my life. But it's still the best thing I've ever done.

The supervisor gave the go ahead to the backhoe operator. He started up the gigantic, cold machine. As the waft of diesel mingled with that newly scarred earth scent, he lifted up the coffin and gently placed Noel Patrick Keane into his final resting place.

It was hard to even open the bottle of whiskey. It was so cold that my hands had gotten numb, my head was cold, and my eyes were blurred. But I was with him and wasn't going to wear gloves or a hat at that moment. If he was going to be in the frozen ground forever, the least I could do was to forbid the elements to win my attention as I honored my dad and his lack of complaining over his last six months while he was poked, prodded, and zapped. I poured a healthy shot of Jameson on top of his casket and cried. I took a generous swig for myself. The burning harshness of the whiskey created warmth and some sort of tribal connection with Dad one last time. I offered the workers a sip; they politely declined. I didn't want it to end, but I could see that they were indulging me. Had I not been there, this would have been a three-minute dig n' dump. I took the shovel, scooped a few loads on top of the wooden box, and stepped back. One last shot of whiskey for him and one for me. One last drink together. With tears streaming and some heavy sobs, I awkwardly signaled to my two new friends that they could finish their task. They covered him in no time. Just like that, he was buried.

In a gesture of compassion, both workers walked over and shook my frozen hands. My job was finally finished. I turned toward Maxie waiting in the running car, *his* car. I gave her a big kiss as she tended to the salty tears on my flush cheeks, and we headed back to our home, *his* home, where my brother Chris was tending to the hungry mourners by himself. Chris and I had just gone through a six-month battle together and were now closer than before. I raced back to my brother's aid.

CHAPTER NINE

"Round Here"
by Counting Crows

Get me the fuck out of here, my mind screamed. It was another brutally cold, wet Michigan day. But my heart was having a hard time leaving. The U-Haul was loaded with Maxie, my only precious cargo, and a bunch of junk to furnish my new apartment in New York. A great job awaited me back in the city at Lespinasse, a four-star restaurant. Finally, my four-star vault was within reach. Dad was buried, the house was sold, and that chapter was closing.

I hadn't settled down since I left high school to go to Cornell. It was simply one move after another in search of my elusive career. I chased the hard work and made memories with strangers in unfamiliar cities that kept me in the dark about my increasing loneliness with all the bustle and noise. I always had Maxie with me, so there was some stability. But I missed my family. Being back in the house with Chris while we cared for Dad was a pretty incredible experience. Mom wasn't physically there due to the messy divorce, but we could reach out anytime. Chris and I handled the day-to-day together with some strong support from Uncle Wayne and Aunt Maureen just down the street.

It had gotten rough a few months back. I was exhausted and at my wit's end as to how to make it any better for Dad. His body was deteriorating, and his mind was slowly slipping, but not fast enough to be unaware of what was happening. It was an awful journey for a powerful man. I would break down from time to time when I was alone and just sob into Maxie's waiting compassion.

Chris was exhausted, too. He was going through a divorce, helping with Dad's care, and holding down the law firm my father had built. And we were fucking broke at the time, too. His stress was palpable, but we bonded together and rededicated ourselves to doing whatever we could to make Noel's life better in those final weeks.

Despite all of the burdens Chris was shouldering during that time, he was there for me, giving me what I needed when I didn't know what I needed. I was struggling with intense guilt because part of me wanted it to be over, and another part of me hated myself for thinking like that. But I just wanted my dad to pass on and move out of this battered shell of a body that once housed my father.

The card appeared on the dining room table next to some flowers one morning after I had finished Noel's injections. I like flowers. My name was on the card.

> I just want you to know that what you are doing for Dad is incredible. He appreciates it, and all of us appreciate it. This would be unbearable without everything you are doing. Hold on; he needs you and loves you. It won't be much longer. Love, Chris.

It was perfect, exactly the motivation I didn't know I needed. He's always been there when I needed help or comforting. He put up with a bratty little brother who pushed for attention nonstop, always showing patience and foresight. The only exception to that rule happened just one time when I deserved a dose of tough love.

He had launched me into the neighbor's bushes on a chilly Sunday evening as we were taking the trash out to the street corner. I believe I had chucked my bag of trash at his head to start the episode, and after twelve or thirteen years of dealing with my antics, he finally snapped. He grabbed me quickly, and quietly tossed me into some soft evergreens. We never talked about it again. The message had been received. I don't have proof, but I'm positive Mom and Dad high-fived him when he came back into the house as I picked pine-like needles out of my jacket and reconsidered my approach to harassing him. He should have beaten me then; I deserved it. But that was the last time we fought. It's a good thing I figured out how to treat Chris better as I grew up. He's been my protector, my consiglieri, and someone I've tried to emulate.

In our final months with Dad, Chris and I were able to find happiness and respite in the mundane turned silly. Even with the grim blanket of Dad's death sentence covering our house, we laughed a lot. We started to gamble on the outcome of Dad's blood sugar read. Winner take all, but only if it was a direct hit on the exact number. Since I controlled Dad's diet, a well-timed glass of orange juice allowed me to steal a few wins. But hey, I wasn't making any income, so don't judge me.

We also pulled off a few little miracles along the way. Even with our bank accounts close to nonexistent, we somehow managed to pull in every favor we could from Noel's loyal group of friends. Mark Campana, an influential yet remarkably down to earth friend, convinced Noel's favorite singer in the world, renowned Irish tenor Frank Patterson, to fly to Detroit and put on a surprise performance for Dad's last birthday. Less than three weeks before he would finally succumb to the illness, we wheeled Dad, clad in a tux, down to Aunt Mo's house and propped him up on the couch with a glass of wine. As I introduced Frank Patterson, Dad's jaw dropped, the first and only visibly shocked reaction I'd ever seen on him. I mean, this man, my dad, never flinched when he was grilled on *60 Minutes* by Mike Wallace for creating the highly controversial practice of surrogate parenting in America. But when he saw Frank, something changed in him. He loved every minute of Frank's performance. Chris and I locked eyes and silently congratulated the other on pulling off the impossible.

Chris confided in me on that chilly, rainy day in Michigan before Maxie and I drove back to New York that he didn't want our time to end either. We were a great team, and it felt like home when we were together. Even though we had just witnessed a brutal battle with cancer, we were both thankful for the time to reconnect. It felt right. Part of me wanted to stay and never leave that comfort. But there were kitchens to conquer, people to meet, and opportunities to create. I think Chris always knew that having each other close was important. But that time back in Michigan seared that wisdom into me.

We made a pact that day to get what was left of our family—Mom, Chris, and me—back together in one place so we could be near each other for the good times and bad. When the rain turned to hail, we knew we'd stalled our goodbye as long as we could. As the hail pelted our faces and the tears ran down our cheeks, we kissed goodbye. I asked him if we could agree to settle somewhere with better weather—soon.

This brief chapter of my life impacted my thinking on my chosen career field in a way I am still trying to reconcile and simultaneously affect in a positive new direction. In a twisted way, I'm lucky Noel got sick when he did. If he had gotten sick when I was at my next job after Lucy's, I'm not sure I would have left. Or, if I had opened my own place at that time, there is no way I could have picked up and left. The business would have died if I had. That's one of the biggest problems in this industry. All people should be able to care for a sick family member. Full stop. But it isn't practical in the hospitality business the way it's structured. I left Michigan with a new set of rules for myself, and I've been trying to impact the industry ever since then with a little success here and there.

CHAPTER TEN

"On My Own"
by Les Misérables Original London Cast

A deep, internal drive lured me back to New York City. I wanted to push myself to see if I could compete and succeed at the absolute highest level in the food world. I had worked at some pretty good places but had not yet reached the pinnacle—a four-star restaurant. I craved, down to my core, to know if I could hang with the best. Even though I wanted to stay home, my ambition won over my desire to be with family. Another bonus to New York was that last call in Manhattan was four in the morning.

About two weeks after we had buried my father, and before I'd left Detroit, I received a voicemail from Chef Gray Kunz from Lespinasse, a four-star restaurant in New York City. Stan, wanted me out of Detroit because he was of the firm belief I needed to be right back in the thick of the intensity and excellence of the big city to find my true potential as a chef. So, Stan had personally hand delivered my resume to Chef Kunz. His message was very sincere in expressing his condolences. I called him back immediately, and when he told me there was a job waiting, I made the decision right then and there that I was going as soon as possible. I actually had the thought that maybe the opportunity arose because my dad somehow aligned the stars to help me out one more time. I was finally going to really learn how to cook.

I had staged at Lespinasse during my previous Manhattan residency.

Equally important, I had eaten there. The food was incredible. I most vividly remember the Black Sea bass with a Kaffir lime sauce. One bite took me to a place I had never been before. It was what food could and should taste like—exotic, unfamiliar, yet pleasing. Everything about that dish was magical. The fish was sweet and moist with crispy skin. The ocean would be proud of how this black bass had been stewarded. The texture and burst of acid from the sauce was otherworldly and included a perfume of something reminiscent and familiar of lime, but at the same time strange and unfamiliar. *What just happened?* I thought. It was by far and away the best thing I had ever eaten, and it was just the fish course. I knew, during that life-changing culinary experience, that I should either work for that chef or quit cooking.

I had been motivated to stage and eat at Lespinasse by Ruth Reichl's four-star review of it in the *New York Times*. I was captivated by the way she wrote about Kunz's culinary genius and weaving of flavors and textures from seemingly incongruous parts of the world in a flawless and unique way. Gray Kunz, the Swiss-Irish guy who grew up hopping through Asia and who cooked at the legendary Chef Freddy Girardet's namesake restaurant, was legit. Salt, acid, bitter, sweet, and umami were artfully woven together on the plates in combinations I had not only never seen before, but with many ingredients I could barely pronounce. *Dorothy, we aren't in Detroit anymore*, I thought. This guy was a culinary genius, and I had to learn from him. (Thanks again, Stan.)

The Lespinasse job offer was technically a step back in terms of position. I could have found a sous chef position or even another chef position at a much lesser restaurant and kept kidding myself that I had what it took to play in the big leagues. But I was confident that stepping back to go and line cook at Lespinasse would give me a leg up for my desired future. Who else would step back in their career and go work a brutal line position for less money and horrible hours just to learn from Gray Kunz? Well, pretty much everyone in that Lespinasse kitchen was in the same boat. They all had a similar epiphany at some point and took a step back so that they could eventually take ten steps ahead.

I had the gift of knowing realistically where I stood in the culinary field. I was a hard worker. I had gotten fast, and I would do anything that was asked of me. I knew I wasn't a stud in the kitchen. I knew I was not a great cook, yet. I had enough experiences by then to know how much more was out there and how much better I could get. I was also honest enough with myself to admit what I didn't know. I was above average. If it was a competition, I would outwork everyone, or I would die before I quit. If I was scheduled to start at eight in the morning I would arrive by five.

Lespinasse was intense from day one. It's hard to describe the feeling of being completely out of my league, emotionally bankrupt to the point of depression from losing my dad, and physically exhausted from working fourteen-hour days. I had not grieved properly yet. I'm still not sure what it means to grieve properly, but my grieving process at the time consisted of crying myself to sleep at night and spontaneously combusting into tears on the subway. Yeah, I was one of those people you don't sit next to no matter how crowded it was or how tired you were. I was hurting. But I had a vison and a goal. I was going to stay the course for at least one year, minimum. I would learn what I could and then reunite with my family after my time at Lespinasse. I just had to stick with it for twelve months. Then, I would be on a path to open my own place near family in San Francisco.

My time at Lespinasse turned out to be love and hate. I wish I could say it was all enjoyable. But most of it wasn't. It really became the epitome, to me, of what is wrong with this business. Let me get this out of the way: Chef Kunz was a brilliant chef. His food was second to none. To this day, I feel and believe that. The technique, the flavor, and the cleanliness of his kitchen were unrivaled. He whipped us into shape like an army of surgeons, with tamarind and lemongrass as our tools. But the atmosphere and work environment were horrible, in my view. There is an infectious and pervasive mentality in the culinary world that a kitchen environment needs to be brutal to be good. You must hurt to create something perfect. You must break the spirits of cooks or employees in order to get them to follow your lead. It almost broke me. But I had promised myself I'd stay one year before I would allow myself to leave. *So, buckle up buttercup. Put your head down, and just work. Eleven months to go.*

Kunz and his sous chef tried to break us in bizarre ways. Fifteen minutes before a Friday lunch service, the sous chef dropped twenty pounds of wild spring onions on my station and told me to have them ready for service. *Fuck you too*, I screamed in my head as he pushed the mess closer to me. There was literally no goddamn way I could do it. No one could. It was easily an hour-long task to clean, trim, and cook. But that was the point, to see if I'd quit. As my face flushed red, and the tears welled up in my eyes, I slammed a stainless-steel hotel pan down on my cutting board to create a little tension and a lot of noise. He wouldn't break me. I would NOT quit. The pan slam was almost asking for the bully to come back and mark his territory by belittling me. The tough guy shot a glance back at me, a warning, and a dare at the same time. I spent the entire lunch manning my station at the stove and running back to my prep area to tend to the onions, barely having them ready as each order came in. I was in a zone and determined. But as I hustled in that kitchen, the sweat running down my temples and dampening my shirt, the question of *why* consumed me. *Why do they want to break me?* There had to be a good reason, right?

I came to realize that there was no good reason for that workplace bullying. Sadly, it was just a cycle of abuse that had been perpetuated for years and was a rite of passage in many chefs' eyes. I think that Kunz, his sous chef, and numerous others like them, believed that that harsh work environment would make the workers tougher. If the workers didn't break, then they would become better, faster, more resilient employees. Maybe that works in the military. Maybe. I'm not qualified to answer that. I do know that we were just making dinner, and the unreasonable demands, yelling, and criticism didn't help us do our jobs.

Even in 1997, the management philosophy of trying to break someone was outdated and defeating. It's what I hated most about

Lespinasse. They relished it when they could get someone to walk out mid-shift. Just think about that for a minute. What type of sadistic fuck wants to hire someone, train them, and then push them to leave in the middle of a Saturday night shift? I'm sorry, but I miss the connection to giving the guests a good experience. It infuriated me at times, almost to the point of quitting before my twelve-month pledge, but I held on. They would not win. I self-medicated with booze, and I made a few great cooking buddies. I cried with Maxie a lot. I remembered I had a plan.

Building people up and inspiring them to work together as a team *for you* and *with you* is always the better way. But too many kitchens like Lespinasse just repeat the abuse cycle. If the chef encourages it with action or inaction, it becomes widespread and toxic. The better and more powerful the chef, meaning more stars and more awards, then the more cult-like the atmosphere in the kitchen could become. The sous chefs serve as enforcers of the great chef's dictatorship. It's trickle-down theory at its best. The underlings will fall on a sword or a bomb for their chef once they drink the Kool-Aid. It's bizarre and dangerous.

It's also very much a male issue. Sure, that's possibly sexist. I can make a strong case that we need more women running kitchens. In my experiences, women tend to lead first by common goal and not ego. They tend to want everyone to succeed instead of taking all the glory for themselves. Us guys, not so much.

I would not trade my time at Lespinasse for anything in the world. I learned how to cook at the highest level. It also taught me a life lesson that would prove itself time and time again over the next few decades; you can learn more form jerks than you do from the good guys. You learn how *not* to do things from the jerks, and you vow that you'll be different when it's your turn to be in charge. During my time there, I vowed that I would be different when my time came. I made it through my year at Lespinasse. I wish that the people who didn't make it through their tours had not been treated as they were. I hope they know they didn't break; they were attacked.

CHAPTER ELEVEN

"I Can See Clearly Now"
by Jimmy Cliff

When my year was up and I had made it through the bullshit the sous chefs had dished out, Lespinasse was in turmoil. Chef Kunz had run afoul of the hotel's union, which then showed everyone that they had the power to effectively neuter him. He was barely allowed in the kitchen, and I could read the writing on the walls; we all could. The inmates were running the asylum. I had learned all I was going to learn in that environment. I had fulfilled my promise to myself by earning my master's degree in cooking in New York City at the highest level. Next, I needed to make good on my promise to my brother that we would get the family back together.

Another early morning hailstorm (see a pattern yet?) was all the final motivation I needed. Right there at the corner 55th and 5th while the hybrid bagel and donut cart was getting set up for business at five-thirty, I decided I was done with New York City. I clocked in at security, changed, and headed up to the kitchen. The mood was particularly miserable that morning. Everyone knew that the shiny toy in the window had lost its luster. The four-star cult that had been created from the critical success was about to vanish. The sous chefs were particularly hostile as their emperor had no clothes, and everyone could see their little johnsons. Corporate hotel management claimed authority. This once empire of cuisine now felt like a dysfunctional family reunion.

"Two weeks. Thanks, guys."

And just like that, I was on my way to the West Coast to get my family back together. Maxie was particularly elated to leave New York City. Minus the occasional pizza and bagel scrap treasures she would score on the street, this city had worn out its welcome with her. Mom was in San Francisco, fully settled, working, and meeting new friends. She was anxiously awaiting her granddog and second born, probably in that order. I promised Maxie beaches, water, parks, and no more snow or cramped apartments.

My heart was convinced that this was the right move, but my ego needed some work. I had just worked at the best restaurant in the best food city in the country, and I thrived there despite all its dysfunction. I could cook with the best of them. But immediately afterward, I was heading to a city that didn't have that culinary stature. And it was damn hard to process that.

An intensity breeds in New York City, permeating everything you do from the second you leave the confines of your apartment. It's worn like a badge on true New Yorkers and on those of us who lived there long enough to get infected. On the streets of New York, getting a cab or buying a bagel is an exercise in social chess. And whatever you do, do not speak to strangers on the street. Walk straight through, don't bump anyone, and don't talk; it's not cool. This intensity isn't entirely a bad thing, though it must wreak havoc on blood pressure, because the atmosphere creates urgency and resiliency—two necessities in the restaurant business.

Even though the truth is that urgency and discipline can be cultivated anywhere, New York City holds an air of contempt for everywhere else in the country. The city seems to suggest that nothing can be as good as the Big Apple. The best of the best and the brightest of the brightest try to stake their claim, and those who succeed land at the top of their games. That's where my head was as my year at the pinnacle of cooking ended. Suddenly, I was in San Francisco without a job, living at my mom's house, and walking Maxie with Mom in Russian Hill.

"What the fuck is their problem?" I scowled to my mom one particular foggy, damp, early morning as we were walking Maxie together and a couple of strangers smiled at us.

"Douglas," she shot back, "they were smiling at Maxie. They wanted to say hi. We do that here. It's nice." She ended the civility admonishment with a familiar movie line from *Mr. Mom*. "Lighten up, Madison Avenue."

I got it. I was no longer in New York City; I could lose the negative intensity. I had decided I'd do things differently upon leaving Lespinasse, after all. I could greet people and enjoy the damp air and the beautiful vistas. It was okay to take it a little slower and a little softer, but it would take time for me to loosen up. To be completely honest, I have never gone fully California in demeanor, but it's nice to know it exists.

CHAPTER TWELVE

"Ho Hey"
by The Lumineers

I carried a recurring dream around with me for a long time. I would walk into the dining room of my own restaurant, and everyone would clap in a spontaneous, but deferred way. As I quietly walked from table to table, I saw that the people were having a great experience. They were thankful and appreciative, but not in a sycophant way. In the dream, it was genuine happiness. I still don't know if that dream was ego or a true manifestation of my initial love of cooking. I wanted to be great at something, and I wanted to make people happy.

I've always felt lucky that I knew what I was meant to do with my life. I had learned early on that cooking, for me, was not a career choice in as much as it was an actual calling—a vocation. I was possibly a natural, born with a great palate, God-given, if that's your thing. At first, cooking gave me an endorphin boost, energy, along with feedback from friends or guests. And once my skill level reached a certain tipping point, I could combine the previous rushes with the new high of knowing it went well. It became a confidence that no one could take away. And it was pure, I think. I wanted to make people happy with food. It felt really honest. The higher up the food chain (in terms of cuisine level) I went, the more rewarding the work felt, as the stakes seemed higher, and the praise came from seemingly more important people. Seeds of corruption? I was too entrenched and young to be that cerebral.

Mostly, I enjoyed the hard work in the beginning. I believed that in order to be successful, I had to work really hard, drop-dead-tired hard, Midwest ethics hard. My parents taught me that ethic. Kitchens were hard work, and the more I sacrificed, the better I got, and the more my soul felt less guilty about all the personal and familial sacrifices. Screw the weddings of my best friends and any kind of vacation; I needed to make dinner.

There was also something creative about cooking that drew me towards the kitchen light. As mentioned, I loved digging ditches and mowing grass as a kid; immediate gratification was always addictive to me. But cooking topped ditch digging with its room for creative expression. Beyond the creative aspect and immediate gratification, the buzz of a kitchen once service began was addictive. I think it's a little like air traffic control, but with steaks and veggies. Orders verbally flew through the air as the hoods roared, oil sizzled in the pans, and the razor-sharp carbon steel Sabatier knife chopped the shallots. But most of all, I could feel the noise inside me. It was the beauty of controlled chaos when done right. It was a peaceful place for me because I could control it. The singular focus required at a cooking station was, to me, bliss. Damn, I was a great line cook. Being in the zone was such a natural high.

"SIX NEW YORK, FIVE HALIBUT, TWO WELL DONE."

"*Oui*, Chef."

The rising temperature and inert pressure created its own weight. It may have been a dead piece of protein I was trying to land on a plate, but it sure felt like a 747 full of lives I was trying to land at JFK, followed by six more right behind it. I was meant to do this work. Most of those people dining had something else to do real soon. That's right, post-dinner drinks with Buffy and Biff. So, I just made it happen absolutely perfectly from six to nine at night.

"*Oui*, Chef!"

Even friends who were pissed off that I couldn't take a weekend off to go to their weddings or their mom's funeral still enjoyed the perks of knowing Chef Douglas—free food, and VIP treatment. Everybody loves a chef. And, I had found something I was pretty damn good at. So, my friends and family respected it, even if it did tire me out. Besides Stan, none of them had any idea how to judge me then. Even so, praise from people, even if I didn't like them, felt great. For the first time in my life, I had some leverage with people, a leverage I felt I needed, and a leverage I badly wanted. I needed them to tell me how good I was. I needed them to admire me and want to be around me, even if it wasn't reciprocal because I didn't want to owe them anything. This was how I began to acquire *leverage*, even though I didn't know it at the time.

When I arrived in San Francisco, I was already a really good cook. The time it takes to achieve that varies, but the reality is that cooking's not that hard; after all, it's just dinner. Repetition is what leads a good cook to greatness. A cook needs to have repeated a skill so many times that she can be mentally inside the piece of meat or fish to feel when it's getting too hot or too hard, but not because it's overcooked.

When you sear a steak, you sear it super-hot and create a crust. The inside of the steak then tightens up because it's reacting to the searing. So, if you don't know what you're doing, you could think that it's overdone. But, over time, the steak will relax inside, whether it's in the pan or resting on a rack outside of the pan. Only then, during that resting period, will you be able to gauge the inside of that steak. You can only learn that by doing it a couple hundred times. There is a subtle difference in touch that takes a while to decipher. When you do, you attain a higher level as a chef. I was at that level during my San Francisco job search.

My ego was a real impediment to landing a job. How would I find a kitchen to call home? Lespinasse was not only a beacon for high-end cooking, but the kitchen was literally spotless and magnificent. The technique was never sacrificed, and the ingredients were the best that money could buy. I realized that I needed to find a home that brought me back to the feeling I had when I first started cooking, and simultaneously to the feeling I felt working at the level that Lespinasse required. And I needed to find a home that would put me on the trajectory toward my dream of running my own four-star restaurant.

Cleanliness was the biggest issue in almost every place I staged in San Francisco. I couldn't get past the fact that they weren't clean—at least not by my standards. Four Seasons was big and busy, and on a Saturday evening it could get a little messy; but it was never dirty. Lespinasse was spotless from dusk 'til dawn. In fact, there were times in the middle of service that Chef Kunz would want to bring a guest back for a kitchen tour, and we would spend ten minutes straightening up an already perfect kitchen while the chef tapped his foot impatiently. It was OCD at its worst, but an incredible way to work. These kitchens in San Francisco were straight-up dirty and messy, and I wanted no part of them. I was *not* going to compromise that standard.

The techniques at many of the restaurants I staged at were unimpressive, too. At Lespinasse, every step was done right. If a dish needed sixteen touches, it got it. The meat and fish were cooked, rested, and basted beautifully with a frothy emulsion of butter and oil, smashed garlic, and thyme. At one particular hot restaurant in San Francisco that the famous critic Michael Bauer had lauded as the latest and greatest, I saw the staff wrap their signature monkfish in lotus leaf at four, put it in a hotel pan, and place it on top of the oven. When a customer ordered the dish, anytime between five and eight or even later, they would throw it in the oven to cook it. An airline puts more thought into the execution, let alone food safety protocol.

After three weeks of checking out potential establishments, I was appalled, offended, and growing a little depressed. I started to rethink whether I could find a cooking home in San Francisco. And what was up with everyone doing bacon-roasted fingerling potatoes with crispy, airline bone chicken breast? The whole city seemed like it had a menu convention and then went back to their establishments and never deviated from what the dear leader had dictated. Needless to say, the creativity didn't impress me.

As my luck with finding a good home to cook at in San Francisco faded, I reached out to Rebecca Chapa, with whom I was pretty close friends in college. We had lots of fun navigating the food and beverage lanes together back at Cornell, and we had both moved to Manhattan immediately after to pursue our crafts. Rebecca was a remarkably talented sommelier at Jardinière. She had been part of the opening team there and, in a short time, had become one of the leading young wine voices in San Francisco. I thought it was a good idea to let her know I was in the city and hoped she would recommend a suitable place for me to land.

Jardinière was on my radar. It was a pretty high-profile, recent opening, featuring Chef Traci Des Jardins and restaurateur Pat Kuleto. But it wasn't the type of place I saw myself calling home. It was in the Ballet and Symphony District in San Francisco, which meant pre- and post-theatre rushes. I was over that part of my life. Beyond the location issue, Jardinière specialized in California food with a heavy French influence. At that time, although I respected the craft of that style, I really wanted to focus on Asian flavors in dishes. They spoke to me in a deep way. But Rebecca said she loved working with Traci because she's real, and the restaurant was doing great. Jardinière was also the right size, not quite as big as Four Seasons but still big enough. So, Rebecca and I agreed that I should meet Traci and do a stagiaire for a night. It couldn't hurt.

I arrived a few minutes early, as always, dressed in a suit. Maybe it's my Midwest upbringing or my East Coast finishing, but I think showing up as professional to any interview is important. A suit says that you take the interview seriously. It was raining heavily that morning. It was the kind of cold San Francisco rain that makes you wonder what the California sunshine is all about after you've relocated from the East Coast.

My first impression of the Jardinière building was that it was strong and comfortable in contrast to the vast majority of the surrounding architecture. Most of the city of San Francisco is cloaked in Victorian architecture. By far and away, my least favorite style of architecture is Victorian. It just seems old, fussy, and ostentatious. I've always thought that Victorian architects just wanted to paint in the lines. I prefer New York City or Hong Kong architecture with its modern, clean-lined, gleaming skyscrapers that are so clearly defined by architects with something to say. I have no idea where or when my architecture snobbery was born, but it exists. It makes no sense at all, but along with my expensive champagne taste and dress shoes, architectural snobbery completes my affected side. So, I argue that while there is plenty of beauty to San Francisco, it's not in its uninspired buildings. I wouldn't say that the building Jardinière was inspired. But there was something real and gritty about the brick exterior. It reminded me of Chicago a little.

Traci Des Jardins is tiny, but her presence isn't belittled by her size. She's comfortable and confident without being cocky. As we were introduced, I could feel that this five-foot-two woman, dressed in a T-shirt and jeans with wet, just out of the shower hair, was wondering what the hell this Ivy League, New York City, suit-wearing guy was doing there. She wasn't rude by any means. I could just tell in that instant that the suit was the wrong choice. It came across as phony to her. The rest of the world sees a suit and tie at an interview as customary and good form. But it's a little overkill for cooking positions, as most cooks don't own a suit and tie. But to me, if that was ever the reason I missed out on a job, I'd have been okay with that.

Chef Traci and I chatted for a few minutes about my goal of finding a restaurant to call home in San Francisco because of the promise I'd made to my family. I was honest about my recent disappointments with other restaurants in San Francisco. I may have sounded slightly arrogant, but there was a certain chemistry or frankness in our discussion that day. It was a real talk. She wasn't dismissive of me by any means, but I could tell by her tone that she wasn't that interested in me. Traci politely let me know that they didn't have any positions available, but that I was welcome to hang out for the night and check things out.

"Sounds good," I replied.

CHAPTER THIRTEEN

"Time After Time" by Cyndi Lauper

A stagiaire is the best way to assess whether a restaurant is a good fit for both the cook and the kitchen. A chef can't assess someone's full skill set in one night, as each kitchen has a unique way of doing things that takes time to learn. But a chef can easily *suss* out who can hang on a busy line and who is worth an investment of time.

The kitchen at Jardinière was a great example of why a restaurant owner should never let a restaurant designer push forward a design without a chef's input. Kitchens need to be efficient, but they also need space to make them work. Restaurant designers, for the most part, tend to focus on the sexy parts of the restaurant, the front of house (FOH). The remaining parts, the guts of the business, fall to whatever square footage is left. Seats make money, and kitchens cost money. It's an outdated and shortsighted way to design. Unfortunately, it's all too common.

I could take one look at Jardinières kitchen and sum up that Traci didn't get much input into the size. Most chefs, desperate to have their own piece of a deal, would say that they could make it work. The truth is, they do make it work, but the bad design and scrimping on space comes with a huge hit on employee wellbeing and the ability to produce. If the design process was more deliberate, it would reverberate in countless positive ways in the industry.

I could tell that Jardinière's kitchen wasn't ideal for the volume they were required to produce, but there was something efficient about it. There was a long, single hot line with an enormous, *stainless-steel pass*, a term of art that describes where the food gets directly plated by the cooks and immediately sent out to the nearby dining room. A small pastry area was set up by the steaming stock stoves, and a decent sized *garde manager* (cold line) backed up to the pot washing area. Upstairs, the dish machine for the plates and glasses was nestled next to a dry goods area that melded into the office. The kitchen wasn't brand new, which was surprising as the restaurant was opened only six months ago. The only walk-in had a faux wooden covering that spoke of a much earlier time.

The physical appearance of the kitchen left me unimpressed. Compared to the million-dollar stainless mecca I left behind at Lespinasse, it wasn't likely that anything would impress me. But here's the thing, this seriously cramped kitchen was clean. The floors, visually unforgiving under the fluorescent lights, were void of any debris, and there was a sous chef sweeping as I entered. A small army of prep and line cooks toiled at a brisk pace, shoulder to shoulder, as they passed finished work to and from each other across the massive, stainless table. The pace seemed serious, but not chaotic. And there wasn't any yelling—*none*.

The product was fresh. The vegetables were gorgeous. It was February, and the Brussels sprouts were bright green. Pungent green garlic was being sliced thin and then quickly butter braised. The baby carrots had an earthy sweetness to them that I had tasted only once before at a farm in Ithaca as they were pulled out of the ground. Ah yes, the obligatory fingerling potatoes were being pan roasted with Hobbs' bacon (try it once and you'll be a convert), surely for the crispy chicken to rest on later that night. At least it was Hobbs' bacon.

I was handed over to Lucas, the fish cook, to help him prep and run shotgun on his station. I could hang with the big boys in New York City at Four Seasons and Lespinasse, so I wasn't intimidated. I would most likely get my chance to show them at some point, but until then, I'd be helpful as directed. Lucas was great, personable, and worked clean. In fact, it seemed everyone worked that way. There was a hustle of energy permeating the atmosphere in the kitchen, but it was met with a jocularity and looseness that was refreshing and didn't detract from the tasks at hand. People seemed happy there, a much-appreciated change from the New York environment.

The sauces were gorgeous and made with lots of French technique and care. The proteins were fresh: local king salmon, Alaskan halibut, lovely sea scallops, and Niman Ranch pork belly. The fish was cooked to order. The meats were seared, basted, and rested perfectly. The technique was flawless, and the ingredients were the best. And the broom kept making an appearance. The thing with a small, cramped kitchen is that if you don't keep up on the tidiness, it can be brutal. Every half hour or so, there was cleaning going on. They were doing the best with what they had, showing pride in the craft, and respecting the techniques of the trade. I was impressed, even if it was French. At least the crispy chicken was crispy and juicy.

As much as I was taking their inventory, I knew full well that they were taking mine. Cooks are competitive, and I was now in their house. Did they want me? I know Traci said there weren't any positions available at the moment, but that had more to do with the Hermes tie and Traci avoiding an uncomfortable situation with Chapa if I sucked. In the culinary world, if someone with talent walks in your door, you find space. There is enough turnover in the staff that it's worth investing time in someone with potential. About an hour into service, Lucas suggested we switch positions. I would cook the protein (fish), and he would be my entremetier (vegetable cook).

Cooking fish, to me, is pure art. It's delicate, needs constant attention, and has a short window of perfection. I much prefer the challenge of fish over meat. With meat, cooks have the luxury of resting it and watching it to attain perfection. But with fish, you better just know. And don't forget to take into consideration the time that it takes the fish to travel to the guest. It will keep cooking. You've got to keep your focus.

I was able to show my skill set over the next two hours. In all honesty, I loved every minute. I was having a blast. The team was young, but they all cared, and they were busting their asses. The end result was really great food with lots of integrity, and I admit with some pain that even the crispy chicken with fingerlings was legit.

Towards the end of service, I saw Traci not so subtly call Lucas over. I knew what this was about. Shortly after Lucas returned to our station, Traci beckoned me over to her corner.

"Something's opened up. We have a position, and I think you would be a good fit."

Never let good talent walk out the door.

I told her I was very interested but would love to talk with her some more as I really wanted a home with some movement for my career. We moved up to the combination office and storeroom to dig deep into career goals. Remembering my previous encounter with Terrance Brennan back in New York City, I strategically charted my emergency exit path just in case espressos started flying. I confided in her that I wanted to be management, that I wasn't afraid to learn the line and spend plenty of time on it, but that I wanted my own restaurant someday. I needed to have some management responsibility in San Francisco if I was going to attract attention and investors.

I let her know how impressed I was with the kitchen, the level of technique, and the happy, team-like environment. I didn't say it out loud, but it was obvious to me that the happiness I had witnessed came from how she treated people, and the respectful tone she set. There was no sacrifice of quality because of the informal, pleasant work environment. Instead, just the opposite occurred. Despite the physical limitations of the facility, and despite the volume, the crew came together and not only overcame the normal impediments, but thrived on it.

My eyes were opening wider every second. Maybe, just maybe, the saying that "you learn more from the assholes" wasn't true this time.

Jardinière wasn't my elusive four stars. It's just not possible to produce four-star food in that quantity. But it was damn close.

Over the course of the next three years as she slowly handed over her kitchen to me, Traci Des Jardins would become one of my closest advisors and mentors. The way in which she carried herself and her philosophies was magical and inspiring. Here was a great cook, producing great food at a very high volume, and she had accomplished all this by treating people with respect. I would not have a career if it weren't for her lack of ego and willingness to trust in me. She had enough confidence to allow someone like me to eventually get attention for the work I was doing. My name was on the menu when Michael Bauer came in to review us. My name was listed as *chef* at events. She didn't need to do that. No other chef would have. She was at peace with her stature in the industry. She didn't need to hog every headline.

Traci realized that if she could trust someone to run her kitchen with as much care as she had, it would allow her to focus on other things with greater overall importance than just dinner. Because of that, Traci was able to establish Jardinière as the restaurant that embraced sustainability, living wages, and health care for domestic partners. These causes might seem commonplace today, but in 1998, they were a visionary's gamble.

Like I said earlier, we need more women in charge. I have a feeling that if more women had been in charge during my culinary evolution, I wouldn't have broken like I did the night of the four-star Bauer dinner.

CHAPTER FOURTEEN

"Take A Chance on Me" by ABBA

My time at Jardinière included a detour that I would label unfortunate if not for the two important relationships that evolved during that brief time. I briefly left Traci to take a chance on the opening of a new restaurant with a couple of old friends, and the time away from Traci made me appreciate her even more. Beyond that, I cemented my relationships with Nick Peyton and Drew Glassel, who would both eventually become my partners and lifelong friends.

I had spent a brief summer break from Cornell after my sophomore year cooking in San Francisco. Not even Stan could have predicted how much the seeds from that summer break would impact my career. The most important connection I made that summer was with Nick. I was working at the Ritz Carlton Hotel. Nick worked the FOH upstairs in the more formal dining room, and I worked downstairs for Chef Gary Danko in The Restaurant. It was a great summer job in that I got more exposure to a professional kitchen, a new city to explore, and I finally cut my ties to Michigan. At that point, I was convinced that I would be cooking the rest of my life.

I liked Nick right away. He was sharp, dressed the part, and carried himself with a positive energy that I like to be around. Nick was handsome with a remarkable resemblance to Clint Eastwood, though nowadays, he tells me he gets compared more frequently to

John Lithgow. But he still looks pretty sharp, in my opinion. Nick is a true FOH people-pleaser, but he has something that many FOH professionals lack, a true knowledge and understanding of food, wine, and the way service should be provided.

Gary and I had also become close friends that summer. He liked my work ethic, and I liked the work I was doing there. His high-pitched and mousy voice, thin moustache, and bald head atop his pear-shaped physique gave him an almost cartoonish presence. But the man was all business. I was willing to jump in and do anything he asked. I was a sponge soaking up any and all tricks of the trade.

I kept in pretty good touch with Gary and Nick while I finished Cornell and moved down to New York City. They would often visit to check out restaurants or pop in for the James Beard Awards, and I would inevitably grab dinner and drinks with them. I thought it would be nice to have an FOH partner like Gary had in Nick, who could bring as much to the table as the chef. They were a great team.

When I was working at Jardinière, Gary and Nick finally landed a place together, named it after Gary, and convinced me to join them as the opening sous chef. Both Nick and Gary said that we were going to push the limits on the level of service and cuisine in San Francisco. It was hard to leave Traci, but I really saw the move as my chance to do four-stars and be the number one guy under Gary. It was an exciting time. San Francisco was buzzing from the first dotcom boom. Money was flowing, and the city was ripe for an opening to test the boundaries of the San Francisco dining scene. I would also have the privilege and honor of assembling a team—the kitchen staff. So, this detour away from Traci made logical sense. Of course, I had no idea at the time how quickly it would all go bad.

The first person I hired for Gary Danko's was Drew Glassell. I had first met Drew on a rainy winter afternoon in San Mateo at the restaurant Viognier when Gary was the chef there, and Drew was one of his cooks. Gary said that Drew and I needed to meet because we were so much alike.

In the highest register Gary could push his voice, which I noticed he did in many business situations, Gary told Drew to sit with us as we were enjoying lunch and discussing the upcoming opening of Gary and Nick's new restaurant.

Drew was fresh faced, tall, and thin with a solid build. Based on his excessively cropped hair cut (Drew looked like he had just had a haircut about fifteen minutes before sitting down), I surmised that he had served in the military. He was dressed in chef whites as he was working a station in the kitchen. It was neither convenient for Drew nor even remotely appropriate that Gary instructed him to sit down during the busy workday. But Gary didn't care.

I could sense from the first second that Drew was uncomfortable with the command to sit. First off, he wasn't a natural for the dining room. His demeanor said it all. He would rather be back in the kitchen cooking. Second, Drew was torn between his duty to cover his station and a direct order from his boss. I liked him immediately.

We chatted about his background in California and in the Marines. He had just finished culinary school, and this was his first professional cooking job. He was more military than California in attitude, and there was something almost Midwest about his personality. I felt a real connection with him, a kind of mutual respect. I had no idea what Drew's cooking skill level was, but talent is a far distant second to attitude in terms of what I look for in people with whom I want to work. I had built a few kitchen teams before, and I had learned that when going into battle (opening and running a restaurant), I wanted people who would take a bullet for the team. Make no mistake; opening a restaurant is a full-on battle, even in the best of situations. It's just *that* hard. Period. The fact that, by the end of our conversation, this Marine wanted to do the hard work of opening a restaurant with us was a stroke of great luck in an otherwise bad situation.

Gary was on the fence about Drew, worried that he didn't have enough experience. So, I'd have to convince Gary that skill can be taught with the right attitude. The second strike, according to Gary, was that Drew was married. Thus, according to Gary, Drew couldn't commit to the hours needed to do the job. This prejudice is prevalent in the culinary world, but I never allowed it in a kitchen that I have been in charge of. I had no doubt that Drew could hang, and I pushed until I eventually hired Drew as my junior sous chef for Gary Danko's. Don't ever let good talent *or* attitude walk out the door.

A funny thing happened on the way to the opening. Nick remained exactly the same guy I had known for ten years—industrious to a fault, charming, sincere, loyal, and sharp. He was fully committed to the endeavor and to Gary as well. Gary, on the other hand, turned into a first-rate prick. I don't know what changed in him, but it was sudden. He began to disappear for days and weeks at a time, leaving Nick and I to open the restaurant on our own. When he was at the restaurant, he treated everyone around him with great disrespect, the stress spewing out of him like a geyser. Pressure can be a funny thing for people. Some rise and some fall. Gary sunk like a dead weight. And he almost took all of us with him.

Beyond Gary's deplorable behavior, the food was uninspired in direct opposition to what he'd promised it would be when I agreed to join him. The food was basically the same stuff he had done in the mid-1980s at The Ritz and at Viognier. He was serving salmon with horseradish crust and dill cucumbers, filet mignon of beef with potato gratin, and trio of *crème brulée* like a goddamn suburban golf club dining room. In twelve years, it felt like he hadn't come up with one new dish.

But even more than the food, I couldn't stomach Gary's behavior. He treated me fine, but he did not treat the cooks well. He exploited their relationship hardships, saying that their bad relationships were the reason for any shortcomings at work. He justified it as a way to motivate them to work harder. But it didn't, of course. He was just a bully. He abused his power. Those were *my* cooks. I hired them, and I was supposed to lead them and teach them. I couldn't allow them to be mistreated on my watch. Gary would dig up something personal about some of the staff by talking to them as friends. Then, I observed,

Gary would pocket that information to use later to criticize the workers when he was feeling the pressure of the restaurant opening.

For example, after one cook confided in Gary that he was having a hard time with his wife, Gary snapped at him during service. "You're behind. Your wife's in your head. You need to figure that out."

Gary also verbally abused Nick in front of all of us. He accused Nick of stealing from him, and of trying to take over the restaurant from him. He even threatened to have Nick arrested. I believe all of that started when Gary realized how much money Nick could make, and Gary wanted Nick out. It was awful. This wasn't a maître d' and chef tiffing it out over a rough service and blowing off steam. This was downright personal and nasty, and it was calculated to undercut Nick for the whole team to see. It broke my heart. Nick, though he looked pale and defensive during these lashings, never engaged with Gary because his top priority was taking care of the guests.

I supported Nick in any way I could. I tried to make it easier for him to communicate with the kitchen, and I made sure that he had whatever he needed to do his job well. I also stood up for Nick in front of Gary and in front of everyone else. The only good news was that Gary didn't hang out much in the kitchen at that point. He had pretty much delegated the kitchen to me.

I remember Gary walking out of the kitchen one time as I picked up Michael Bauer's entrées on his third and final visit for our *San Francisco Chronicle* review. Two filet mignons, one medium and one medium rare. I assumed Bauer was simply testing whether we could cook them to the right temperature. *Please child, stop. I got this.* Gary's team had been busted for miscooking Bauer's meat at his other restaurant, Viognier, and I guess the pressure was just too much for him that night. I cooked and plated the two perfectly cooked pieces of beef, thank you very much.

Instead of coming over to check them as any half-decent chef would have, Gary walked out of the kitchen muttering something like, "You better get this right."

I wondered at that point if Gary knew how to cook medium and medium-rare without stabbing the meat with a thermometer. He hadn't been on the line in a while. I understood; but *come on*. Walking out of the kitchen? *Please.*

To get through that terrible time opening Gary Danko's, Drew and I often took breaks by running huge containers of ice up the stairs to the roof to dump it in the swamp cooler so that the guys in the kitchen could get a burst of fresh, cool air as a reward for working so hard. We took advantage of those private moments to discuss our frustrations with Gary and with the new restaurant. I also told Drew of my dream to open a perfect, four-star restaurant. My restaurant would focus on putting out truly exceptional, cutting-edge, inspired food. I'd take the time to do things right. I shared with him my appreciation for the cuisine they were producing at Jardinière in much higher numbers and also inspired him with my stories of New York City where I had touched true perfection at Lespinasse and many of the places where I staged.

Drew shared my passion for trying as hard as one possibly could to get it right. He, too, wanted to be the best one could be or get as close to perfection as possible. So, although Drew didn't start out with four-star dreams, by the time we'd worked together for just a few months, he shared my vision. I taught him about how far we could go in the industry. If culinary ambition was a drug, then I was Drew's new dealer.

One day not long after Bauer's visit, Gary slammed a big wooden board right near the cooks "to wake them the fuck up.," as he said to Drew and me later. These guys had been working twelve-to-fifteen-hour days, half off the clock, because they were so dedicated to the opening of the restaurant and to their craft. Gary had come up from the basement and apparently didn't like the energy in the kitchen at three in the afternoon, two hours before service. So, in all his masculine might, he decided to slam the six-foot wooden board we used to slide the plates over during service. I was stunned. The board came close to hitting Drew and another cook, Cobra. I was livid. I wanted to hit Danko right there. But I didn't. I think I was in shock. In all my time witnessing and putting up with abusive bosses in New York, I'd never seen anything like this. In my mind, there's a fine line between verbal and physical abuse. Maybe that's not correct thinking. But I always felt I could walk away or scream back when someone yelled at me. Yelling was one thing still common in the industry back then; physical threats crossed a line.

Gary slithered out of the kitchen after his hissy fit. He knew he was wrong, but he did not apologize. I resolved that I would get through service that night because that's what we did, but I was not going to tolerate any more abuse targeted at the people I could protect.

The next morning, I told Drew that he had a home with me whenever he wanted. I would make room for him in any kitchen I had and would like to work with him again. Then, I asked him to join me with Gary. I wanted a witness.

"I'm out of here," I stated. "I'll give you two weeks. But if you ever threaten or actually harm another person while I'm here, I will deal with you directly, and then I'll walk out. Last night was disgusting, and I won't ever put up with that again."

Gary tried to brush it off and say that we could discuss it later when we were alone.

I let him know that Drew was there on purpose and that we didn't have anything else to discuss. "Two weeks. Got it?"

Part of me fears that I would have ignored Gary's abusive bullshit if the food was truly cutting edge as had been pitched to me. If the food was that great, would I have restarted the cycle I'd experienced at Lespinasse, but as one of the goons? I mean, I had compromised my principles at Lespinasse to learn from a genius. I had justified that it was worth it to see that abuse because I was learning. But I wasn't in charge at Lespinasse. I was pretty much in charge at Gary Danko's, and that may be the piece that saved my soul. I couldn't be responsible for the way Gary treated his employees or his partner—not even a little.

I reached back out to Traci and let her know I wanted to come back if she would have me. We discussed how I could come back as the chef and expand the menu a little with a hint of the Asian ingredients I loved. It was a done deal. I would be back in a month.

I pulled Nick into the bathroom, looked him straight in the eye, and said, "Nick, I don't think you're long for this place. And I'm going to open a four-star restaurant at some point in the future. I would like nothing more than to have you as my partner."

I needed him to know that I saw all of his good traits and that I trusted him and would be honored to call him my partner. We shared a long hug and a few tears before we left our office. I didn't expect an answer about joining up. In fact, I didn't ever really expect him to join me. He was in a different league. He was the Sirio Maccioni of the West Coast, and I was just a young gun from Detroit with no track record of ownership in the big leagues. But he knew what I was made of since we had gone through hell together.

I had witnessed Nick put up with unspeakable humiliation. At the time, I didn't understand why he accepted it. Eventually, I learned that Nick had raised most of the money for the restaurant, and he felt a strong obligation to see the distributions paid to the investors. The restaurant was doing well, but Gary wouldn't let any cash go out in the beginning. Nick was waiting until the investors got paid back. It was another stand-up move by Nick that I'd only learn about much later in our relationship.

As I write this book, Nick Peyton and I have opened ten restaurants together as partners and have had a great time doing it. *Make wise decisions, young Jedis. Go to war with people who have your back.* Nick not only had my back, but when he reached out to accept my offer as a partner a year after our bathroom summit, he gave me legitimacy. He was the seasoned proven pro teaming up with the young buck. People took notice. *Good decision, Chef.* After I left Gary Danko's, I heard from numerous people that Gary liked to refer to me as "nothing more than a glorified prep cook." Hmm, at least I cook.

Even though the time at Danko's was miserable, I still have to appreciate that the experience forced me to take a stand on employee treatment in the culinary workplace as I promised myself, I'd do after Lespinasse, something that has become a cornerstone of my business model and of my ethics. We try hard to produce a healthy environment. We fail at times, I'm sure. But it's helpful to have a guiding light. Beyond that, I gained an even greater appreciation for how Traci ran her restaurants, and I got Drew and Nick. These silver linings would eventually save me after I hit rock bottom.

CHAPTER FIFTEEN

"Lola"
by The Kinks

I took the promotion to chef and headed back to Jardinière. One more step up the culinary ladder and out of public relations obscurity. With Traci's generosity, I was finally able to get noticed and pave the way for my own restaurant while I shepherded hers. It felt really good to be home. There isn't a huge age difference between Traci and me, but she took on a somewhat maternal role in fostering my career. She was selfless, and I logged that memory for my future interactions with young cooks.

Before long, Drew joined me at Jardinière. I put him on the line, and he learned how to line cook at an extremely high level. He was able to help set a New York pace. Together, we created New York speed and focus without the ego and bullshit. It was also nice to have someone's ear to bend in the trenches to see if I should put that crack pipe away every now and then.

"Drew, should we slice a fresh white truffle in that cocktail for New Year's Eve?"

"No fucking way, Chef."

The chef part was added to mitigate the harshness of his appreciated honesty.

As I write this book, it's been over twenty-one years, eight restaurant openings, and nine restaurants total in which Drew and I have worked side-by-side at the stoves. We've been there for each other through one parent death, five dog deaths, three divorces, two marriages (his and mine), the birth of Drew's two daughters, countless beers, five lawsuits, and lots of sweat mingled with success. It's more than a friendship, and it's more than a professional relationship. It's very much like family, but it's family I can bring into battle. In one breath, we can discuss the need to reduce the food cost or to switch up the menu a bit, and in the next, I can ask him through heavy tears to swing by and help me lift Finnegan, my loyal white lab, into the car for his final vet visit. Drew not only helped get me through that deep loss, but he also covered for me at the restaurant and told me to take all the time I needed. As I'm sure you realize, that would never have happened at Lespinasse.

As I slowly but surely assembled my dream team, I had my sights set on the next step and was on a mission to get there. Traci had given me the finishing school I needed. I could cook before, but I was even better now. She had taught me about seasonality and the powerful California ingredient ethos. But most importantly, she had shown me how to treat coworkers the right way and that would be an invaluable gift.

I had to say goodbye to Maxie before my time at Jardinière had ended. The beautiful seventeen-year-old, one-good-hip wonder had taken me as far as she could. She had stayed with me through high school, college, New York, my dad's death, and my transition to San Francisco. She held out as long as she could.

As we lay down on the floor at the veterinary office after her legs had finally quit, she licked my salty tears one last time and seemed to say, *"You got this."*

I could only thank her for being the best friend I could have ever had as she exhaled deeply and released her muscles into my cradling arms.

I mourned her loss deeply for a few months, not sure if I could or should do it again. But the emptiness caused by her absence grew too much, and I started to search the internet for Labrador rescues. Traci, a true animal lover who hugged me and told me to take the day off after Maxie left, busted me for using the computer at work one day.

"Not the typical porn sites I'm used to catching my staff on, Doug," she joked.

I set my sights on a stunningly beautiful, muscular, female chocolate lab whose misfortune seemed to be a tail that was about half her body weight and perpetually injured form her wagging it so often in her cement cell. This caused a vicious cycle of blood to spurt in machine gun rapidity when she saw a friendly face. This was too much for all the other people who had visited her. This was just perfect for me. I named her Lola. I would fix her tail, and she could fix my heart.

Soon after I adopted Lola, Nick reached out to me and said he was ready to start a restaurant together. Things were falling into place. So, we set out on our mission to find a home for our four-star dream. Drew, Nick, and I were an unstoppable team. Lola and I moved up to the town of Geyserville in Sonoma County and into a great home on the beautiful T-T (T-Bar-T) vineyard. I still can't believe I had the honor of living on that majestic land. I vividly remember pulling up to the house with Lola and the moment my feet hit the dirt. A sense of connection to the earth rushed through me with its peaceful energy. I emptied my pick-up truck, opened a bottle of rosé, and watched the most magnificent sunset over the six-hundred-acre vineyard with Lola as the coyotes serenaded us with their melodic howls. In that moment, I knew I was home.

CHAPTER SIXTEEN

"Sweet Home Alabama"
by Lynyrd Skynyrd

I had known for a while that Wine Country was where I should be, but not because of my love for wine. *Shhh*! I can appreciate the beauty of what's made here, but I prefer cheap beer and French bubbles. Rather than the wine, it's the dirt and the land that calls me like a siren. The proximity to fresh vegetables and fruits intensifies the ability to cook a great meal. The road less traveled directly translates to better flavor. Moreover, the weather in Sonoma County is perfect for growing and for living. The landscape is stunning, a postcard come to life. I've never before worked in a place where people are happy to give you three hours of their time to cook them a meal. In Wine Country, the people appreciate the dining experience as the entertainment for the night. There's no show to catch, no party to go to, just dinner. The longer the better.

I didn't have much knowledge of Sonoma County when I first arrived. Coming from Michigan and New York, most of what I had heard about was in the context of Napa Valley. Of the two wine producing regions, Napa owned the marketing mantle for sure. I assumed I would end up in Napa. Traci Des Jardins was the first person to suggest that I look at Sonoma County instead. In retrospect, it's illuminating that Traci subtly pointed out that I would like Sonoma better than Napa. She saw the many coats of lacquer and veneers in

Napa Valley and knew I'd be a better fit in Sonoma County because of its land, agriculture, and people.

Sonoma grows vegetables in abundance, whereas the land has become so expensive in Napa that most of the farms have been pushed out for vineyards. Sonoma has much more land and diversity of terrain. Sonoma has cattle and dairies. The birthplace of *Farm to Table* is Sonoma County. I can pick Gail's Dry Creek peaches, crumble some Redwood Hill Farm goat cheese, and snip some basil from Tucker Taylor's garden in the morning to create perfection on a plate. If I want to go all-out, I can just slice some Journeyman Meat Co. salami on it to take any restaurant guest to the pearly gates. And that's just the salad course. Yes, Sonoma County is my dream restaurant home.

As the opportunity for Cyrus, our dream restaurant, presented itself in Healdsburg, Nick and I jumped at it. Nick, a city boy, held onto a bit of reluctance, but still fully committed. But, like many restaurant openings, Cyrus was taking a bit more time and money than our personal savings accounts could sustain. To buy more time and earn a living, we decided to open a casual neighborhood restaurant in St. Helena, Napa Valley, just a short jaunt over from my vineyard home in Geyserville via the lovely vineyard vista-lined Highway 128. St. Helena, and Napa in general, was overrun with high-end restaurants. So, we settled on a neighborhood restaurant with simple comfort food prepared with attention to detail but without pretentiousness. We decided to call it Market and keep it casual enough that it could run without our daily participation once we got Cyrus opened. We wanted to create a very affordable locals place that could be woven into the fabric of the community.

Unfortunately, Market was not initially greeted with open arms by the Saint Helena locals clad in Lulu Lemon and khakis.

"Who are these guys? Where did they come from?"

"You won't ever be successful with pickles like *this*."

Note that the delivery of that line was accompanied by a sharp tilt of a blond ponytail head down as the woman adjusted her Dolce sunglasses to make eye contact from just above the rims.

"I'm from Chicago, and so I *know* ribs. These aren't crispy enough!"
Chicago? Ribs? Crispy ribs? Dear God, really?

"I'm not going in there until they put my wine on the list."

"Don't charge the locals corkage, but *do* charge the tourists," a gray-haired man with a comb-over said with his finger pointed at me like he was giving me sound business advice I should feel lucky to receive from him.

I was shocked. Did he expect me to administer a residency test at the door?

As someone who has spent considerable time in both Napa Valley and Sonoma County, and in quite a bit of this great country, let me lay down a marker for you. Saint Helena is, in my opinion, the most entitled city in North America. It could be its own chapter, but I won't do that to you. Just a few more sentences. In Saint Helena, I've seen the epitome of privilege. The *haves* do not want the *have nots* anywhere near their White paradise. They also do not want to step out of their comfort zones. It's never fair to lump people from one place into one big pot. There are some wonderful people in Napa Valley, for sure. I will bet a year's wages that the good people with soul and conscience will worry I'm writing about them here, and the true assholes won't even second-guess themselves. The elitists can take a million selfies and still not see themselves.

Napa locals see themselves as superior to Sonoma to such an extent that anything on the Sonoma side of the county line off of Highway 128 can't be any good. In their minds, the deeply rooted, blue-collar agricultural ethos of Sonoma County is the ugly stepsister to the manicured Disneyland-like wineries of Napa. In reality, Napa Valley should thank Sonoma County for growing the food they are able to serve in their restaurants and wineries.

At a small charity dinner Nick and I were cooking at Tor Kenwood's house in between Napa and Sonoma, we announced that we were finally opening our dream restaurant, Cyrus. The ten or so people clapped with enthusiasm. When they inquired where the restaurant would be located, and we replied Healdsburg in Sonoma County, the same people booed loudly. These were real, *How could you?* boos and *We thought you were one of us* boos. Those boos further fueled my resolve to make Cyrus the best.

CHAPTER SEVENTEEN

"Ironic"
by Alanis Morissette

We were all working like dogs. Drew and his future wife, Cynthia, moved in with Lola and me. It was an intense time, but we had a lot of fun, too. Sick days were for pussies or just other careers. *Work. Work. Work.* It had been drilled into me by Mom and Dad, the entire state of Michigan, Stan, and every cook I met along the way. I had it down. I could always sleep on Tuesday, and I knew how to use booze, caffeine, and various meds to get through.

I did find time to take Lola for walks up the hill early in the mornings. During the previous six months of construction of Market, she went to work with me every day. I loved that period of my life. They were twelve-hour days with a long but beautiful drive home. Lola loved the truck, and she was also fond of Les Misérables and '80s and '90s rock. So, the drive time flew, but even if it didn't, we were together. Her gorgeous, loving stare was everything to me. My time with Lola made the lack of work-life balance bearable. I even enjoyed it.

So, the weird twitching in my leg didn't really alarm me. I mean, it was pretty annoying, especially when I was driving. I almost had to stop and pull over a few times. I likely *should have* stopped driving a few times. But that would have made me late for work or late to get home and hurry off to bed so I could get back and work the next day.

So, no pulling over for me. I just twitched and drove.

The first time the leg twitch became a little obvious was on the line at Market. I was cooking sauté. I liked cooking sauté. I loved being a line cook. Drew was running the expo station while Ray and Richie were with me on the line. Out of nowhere, my right leg started kicking uncontrollably. It kicked so hard that I fell back into the wall. Even after the collision, I couldn't stop my leg from flailing and violently kicking.

Since we were in the middle of dinner, and my leg lunges were in the way of executing the line of tickets, Ray and Drew did what any cooks would; they jumped on my leg to stop it. They both grabbed my leg to hold it down. Sure, it probably doesn't make sense to you right now reading this. It made no sense to us at the time either. Cooks just get shit done. But Ray and Drew couldn't stop my leg. It lifted both big guys right up in the air.

Drew tried to assert some order to the chaos unfolding by shouting out, drill sergeant-like, "Hold it down! Push it down!"

I could smell my halibut in the pan caramelizing, close to needing my attention. But damn it! Recognizing my panic over my fish (as opposed to my leg), Ray jumped in and finished the halibut. Drew and Nick dragged me over by the stairway and lay me down. Then, at some point, it just stopped.

Drew brought me a banana and a bottle of orange Gatorade that he must have had in his ass since I had never seen one in the kitchen before that time. Drew was convinced that I needed potassium and carbs. Dehydrated no doubt, right?

Doctor Nick had other thoughts about my diagnosis. He decided that I must have been sitting on my wallet and that the imbalance threw my back out somehow. Also, he advised that I should stop the Xenadrine weight loss pills I was using as legal speed before service so I could work sixteen hours straight. *Huh,* I thought. Maybe he's onto something?

I did agree that day to stop the Xenadrine habit. It seemed logical. But I hated to tell him that I didn't have a wallet. We pushed that event aside the minute it was over, and I'd agreed to stop the legal speed. I also made a real effort to hydrate properly.

A few weeks later, I was in the office upstairs in the restaurant. The aroma of cooking bacon wafted up from the kitchen as I worked on the computer. Suddenly, my right leg again started twitching. It started with a tingle and then moved quickly onto kicking. It had become common then, usually the same kicking, and then it was over soon after it started. Most incidents weren't too drastic, with the halibut caper cooking episode being the outlier. But that morning in the office was different. It was *powerful*. As I sat, unable to move of my own will, *SMACK*, my leg thrusted into the underside of the desk with such force that it lifted the desk off the ground. I was sitting, but the chair was rocking backward, and the desk was being lifted by the force of my uncontrolled leg movements. For the first time, I was scared. I tried to call for help to the downstairs kitchen, but I couldn't talk or even get enough air in my lungs to breathe normally, as if in a nightmare. I started to sweat, but I felt ice cold. I was somewhat paralyzed in fear, a mere witness, while my leg, animated on its own, seemed to be in control. I grabbed the armrests, attempting to stabilize and regain control. But I could neither scream nor get out of the chair. I gasped for air. For a full five minutes, I watched, transfixed, as my leg created chaos. It was the first time in my life that I had absolutely no control over a situation, and I was in true panic. I didn't know how far it could go. When it was over, I was drenched in cold sweat and in a true state of shock.

Nick walked into the office a few minutes later and found me staring, wide-eyed, mouth open. I had moved the chair away from the desk, and I was bent over and pale, with sweat dripping off of my nose.

"What happened?" he asked.

"I couldn't stop it," I replied. I told him everything, beat by beat.

He insisted I go see a doctor. I knew I had to go, but it didn't even occur to me to go to an emergency room or to any doctor immediately while I was at work. My mind was racing, trying to figure out how I could fit a doctor's visit in on my next day off. It still makes me cringe remembering this. Even after that terrifying moment, I was way more worried about how I would find the time to see a doctor than I was about the fact that something was seriously wrong with my health.

It took a few weeks and some bad referrals, but I eventually ended up at an appointment with a neurologist. After three minutes and not much more than a reflex test on my knees, he informed me that I had something on the left side of my brain that needed to come out."

I was forced to make a phone call.

"Hey, Mom. Can you drive me to an MRI?"

I had developed a pretty good ability to read MRI scans during my dad's bout with melanoma. So, while I was in the little tube-like picture coffin, I caught a glimpse through the little security peep hole mirror in the MRI machine. I saw a circular, golf ball size mass on the brain. I asked the tech how it looked, knowing full well he couldn't tell me, as only a doctor could deliver any news. But I wanted to see if that mass on the screen belonged to me or the unlucky bastard in the next room.

The tech's reply was telling. "When are you going to see your doctor?"

"Couple weeks," I replied, finally smelling a little leverage in my pocket.

"What are you doing today?" he asked.

"Driving back to work in Sonoma. I need to get back to work."

"You're driving?" his voice cracked.

"Yep." I owned his ass now.

"Umm, our doctor might be able to talk with you today," he said. "Let me check."

Shit, I thought. *Definitely not the other bastard's golf ball. I hate golf.*

Mom and I got the official diagnosis within the hour. *Brain Tumor. Surgery. Now.*

Ha! I knew Drew and Nick had been wrong. I had plenty of electrolytes, and I was well hydrated. To be fair, the Xenadrine could have caused some problems. But the leg twitching, visually comparable to an image of a dog dry humping another dog at the park, was actually seizures. *Focal seizures*, to be exact. And it was happening because a giant tumor was pressing on the motor pathway on the left side of my brain.

At least I could stop drinking the Gatorade that Drew was forcing on me as a substitute for my vicious Diet Coke habit. Silver linings are important.

We called my brother, Chris, from the car. I think all of us were still in a little shock, having lost my dad a few years earlier.

"I'll be on the first plane," Chris said, without missing a beat. "See you tomorrow."

I actually went to work that night. A good friend in San Francisco was in the process of opening a restaurant, and I had promised to help with his test dinners. So, I worked. The reality of the tumor hadn't gelled, and work was therapy. Then, a lot happened fast.

Stan called in a few favors to get me an appointment with Dr. Mitchell Berger, a real god. Surgery would be in one week. I made Mitch give a prognosis. I wanted all of the information. With a lot of caution, as he could not know for sure until he cut it, he said it looked like third stage glioma. *Fuck. That's not good.* Just FYI, if you ever get a brain tumor and a choice to pick a team, pick meningioma over glioma. A glioma prognosis entails chemotherapy and radiation. I don't look good bald; I tried it when my dad got sick. Also, a diagnosis of third stage glioma does not have a great survival rate. You get about five years to live with treatment. Damn; I hated the internet with all its free information. I much preferred the dog rescue sites.

I had seven days to get my thoughts together. I remember coming up with *contrition without submission.* That's how I'd proceed. But even more than sifting through my emotions and strategizing a plan, I just wanted to go see Lola. Who was going to take her while I was in the hospital? We had basically just gotten together and become a family. She could not go back to a kennel; I wouldn't allow it. I needed to see Lola.

My buddies flew in for the surgery—Tony, Robbie, and Mario. Chris was, of course, already there. We all hung out for a weekend before the knife festivities on Monday morning. Traci stopped by, too, and we cried together. I admitted to her that I was scared. The Bromleys were there, as always. If it wasn't for Stan, I would never have gotten in to see Dr. Berger on such short notice. Stan had pulled a rabbit out of his hat, as usual. Aunt Mo flew out from Michigan, still mourning the loss of my dad, her brother.

I felt bad for Mom. Real bad. I never had children of my own, but I could understand the emotion of a parent having to endure that kind of fear. And I cried for Lola. Her tail was finally fixed. I didn't want her to be alone again. No more concrete floors. No more cages.

The boys went to a strip bar the night before the surgery to blow off a little steam. A strip bar, God bless 'em. I got up early and went to the ocean with my mom, Chris, and Lola. I wanted to see the sunrise. I knew I needed to make peace with the fact that what I was facing was life-threatening. But no way in hell was I giving up. I held onto my hope. I called Stan, Judy, and Aunt Mo. I told them all that I loved them and then tried to deflect from the gravity of it all by telling them that they should all drink a lot at my funeral. *Contrition without submission.*

We went to the hospital after a particularly rough goodbye with Lola. She knew. Of course, she did. The boys showed up to the hospital a little late, hungover, and in need of food. But they showed up. This was tough on them, too. Mingled somewhere in between lines of jocular banter, a heavy seriousness weighted the conversation. After a couple of hours, Chris broke down and took the guys for greasy eggs across the street to ease their hangovers. Ironically appropriate for our relationships, Chris and the boys all missed saying a final goodbye to me before they wheeled me into surgery. Those guys didn't need to be told to drink a lot at my funeral, so we didn't really need to do the goodbye thing anyway.

Mom held my hand when they wheeled me into a new super clean, super bright room.

"I love you too, Mom," I said as the nurses wheeled me through the operating room doors. "Sorry."

The anesthesiologist, a jovial guy, started explaining that he was about to give me the equivalent of a whole bottle of Pinot Noir plus a little, he paused for effect, "if you shot-gunned it."

Sounded good to me. It smelled cold, and it felt cold. The lights were painfully white.

"Count backwards please," he said.

But instead of counting, I asked, "Mitch, do you need a break? A snack?"

"I'm fine, thanks," he laughed.

"What type of music do you want to play?" I asked. "I watch *ER*, you know."

"Do you want music?" he asked. "I can get you music."

"Oh no, I want YOU to be comfortable."

He laughed. "I'm fine, Doug."

"Did Harvard used to lose to Cornell in football when you played for Harvard?" I blurted out in whatever defiance I had left. No submission.

He laughed again. "Uh, no."

There is nothing like trying to piss off your brain surgeon right before surgery. But I ran out of things to say. So, I started counting backward from one hundred.

Though I couldn't count for long, I remember my thoughts clearly. *Will I see Dad? Chemo looked awful, but he never complained. Do I believe in God? Lola! Maxie and Dolly . . . will I get to see them again?* The feeling I experienced when I saw my dad in his casket overcame me. I still hadn't dealt with my emotions. I hadn't made time for it. In that brief moment, I made a resolution. *If I wake up, I'm not going to be the same insanely driven guy who can't take a day off. I'm going to slow down, take care of myself, and maybe even properly date somebody.*

Contrition without submission.

CHAPTER EIGHTEEN

"I'll Fly Away"
performed by Gillian Welch and Alison Krauss

I remember waking up in sensory steps. My first sense to register was smell. Before I could open my eyes or even hear anything, I was overwhelmed by an odor I can only describe as something akin to burnt tires and rubbing alcohol. The second sensation that awoke in me was pain; I'd never before or since experienced such agony. It was a pounding, throbbing pain, and it was unbearable.

"WAKE UP," some asshole shouted. "WAKE UP."

The volume of his demand amplified the pain in my head, and my body responded with retching, then vomiting.

"WAKE UP."

Fuck you pal; this hurts. I tried to open my eyes to catch glimpses of my surroundings. *Who the hell is yelling at me?* But I couldn't keep my eyes open for more than a second or two at most.

In one moment of vision in between vomiting spews, I spied the nurse at my bedside. She was cute. I channeled my Irish wit.

"This," I managed to say with labored breath, "is, by far, the worst hangover ever."

In the most intense emotional moments in life, I tend to crack jokes. The more ill-timed the better. This one wasn't my best material, but I had just had brain surgery. I'm pretty sure I got a smile, and she did eventually go out on a lunch date with me. This system had worked well for me in many situations; deflection without reflection.

For example, the morning I found out that Anthony Bourdain had committed suicide, I texted my best friend, Lance. "I hear CNN has an opening." Then, a second later, I sent, "Too soon?"

I knew I could get Lance to laugh; that was easy. He's often willing to go deep into the gutter of inappropriateness with me; most of my best friends will. Lance was the only one who laughed at his twins' baby shower when I gave him a box of condoms during gift opening time. But I did this (and I think we all do) because I couldn't communicate how deeply sad I was. I couldn't communicate how Bourdain's death was far too close for comfort. I couldn't communicate my deep fear that he and I might be cut from the same depressed cloth. Deflection without reflection. That character trait would eventually lead me, in great part, to my emotional cliff dive the night of the four-star Bauer dinner. Because I was so used to using deflection as a crutch, it makes sense that I whipped it out post-surgery during one of the most intense moments of my life.

They wheeled me into the noisy, glaringly bright hallway and then into the ICU. My mouth felt like sandpaper. I felt like an elephant had sat on my head and put his trunk all the way down my throat.

"The morphine's not working for his pain," someone said.

No shit, guys!

"Maybe he's allergic."

I'm right here, pal.

"Okay, Douglas," said the asshole who had just been screaming at me to wake up.

He wasn't cute.

"I'm going to give you this shot of Dilaudid," he said. "First, you are going to feel a real cold in your chest, and then you'll feel heat all over."

He administered the drug.

HOLY SHIT! Instantaneously, life was good!

I've always known I have some type of addictive personality. That's why I stayed away from the more addictive drugs. But in that post-surgery moment, in the seconds after I got the shot, I instantly wanted another shot of Dilaudid. It was incredible. I understood for the first time what a heroin addict experiences.

Could I have a beer chaser? I wanted to ask.

I could barely enjoy my pain free moments because all I could think about was how to get more, more, more. I did eventually con one more out of them the next day, but I think they realized what was going on and cut me off cold turkey after dose two.

I wonder now what would have happened if I had somehow had the ability to cut myself off from the drug of the four-star dream and all of the accompanying accolades. The problem with that is that I believe in my core that working hard and striving to be the best is inherently good. And it can be good. Problems arise when I depend on the critics to tell me (and the world) if I'm good enough, if I've reached the apex of my profession. I've tried to kick my critic affirmation addiction many times. I have successfully, from time to time, stopped myself from reading social media reviews, cancelled magazine and newspaper subscriptions, and even told colleagues that I would not look at the reviews as a way to get accountability at work. Sometimes, I break down and peek. Like I said, I'm an addict. But I'm working on it.

Dr. Berger came by to tell me that he thought he got it all, he didn't think it was stage three glioma, but he didn't know what it was. We wouldn't find out the answer for about three more weeks.

Those three weeks in between surgery and diagnosis, mostly in the hospital, were pretty intense. I couldn't feel or move my toes. I couldn't walk without a walker and a bunch of help. I was jacked up on steroids and crying at the drop of a hat. *Poor me. Poor me.* One day, it hit me. I should have studied harder in college. I had relied on my body up until then, and its limitations had become apparent, seeming out of nowhere—except that I knew it wasn't out of nowhere. My body had been giving me signs for a long time. I feared that my body might not allow me to work in a kitchen again. *Holy shit!* I was just getting started. I didn't know anything else. *More importantly, I'm good at cooking, the best damn line cook in North America.* How would I walk Lola? I missed her something awful.

My resilience pushed me through those thoughts and my recovery. I knew I wasn't done yet. I needed to cook. I had something to prove to the world. The whole setback of the brain tumor just pissed off this already angry Irishman. I emerged much more determined. But hanging over my head was a big dark reality that I wasn't ready to deal with; I still couldn't walk, and I didn't know if I would walk again.

I cried with joy when the feeling came back to my toes. I had been working so hard, physically and mentally, to push the pathways clear. When those nubbly, bad-nailed, ugly toes finally wiggled, it was the breakthrough I needed.

I wanted to show them I wasn't dead . . . yet. So, Mom and I drove up to Saint Helena, and she wobbled me in for lunch at Market. It was so good to see everyone, and it was so lucky that the good news of my diagnosis came during that lunch when I was surrounded by family and friends.

Dr. Berger called my flip phone cell. It was a meningioma, which is a good team to get drafted by as opposed to team glioma. I wouldn't need chemo or radiation. Damn. Luck of the Irish. No chemo. No radiation. And likely no more surgery even if it did grow back. I'd just need a bunch of physical rehabilitation to get walking again on my own.

I worked my ass off to get better. Lola and I moved back up to the T-T property and started to walk. And sleep. And recover. You might be thinking that I would have gotten reflective then and slowed down a bit as I had promised myself just a few months ago as I lay counting down for surgery. But I was hell-bent on getting back to work, and most importantly opening Cyrus. I was on a mission. I had something to prove.

You never know what makes rebels tick, but everyone loves freedom. So sang James Connolly when referring to the IRA who fought for their freedom. But at some point, the fight became about pride and ego, too. Some people have a huge ego and don't know it. I don't know if my refusal to slow down and my resilience to push harder and harder, even after the tumor, came from my work ethic and the feeling that I was meant to cook, or if it was really my ego propelling me. But on I fought for success, again disregarding my body's pleas to work differently and with more balance in my life. This disregard for my physical and mental health would continue to take its toll over time, and it eventually steered me to the road of self- destruction the night of the four-star dinner.

CHAPTER NINETEEN

"Landslide" (Acoustic) by Fleetwood Mac

Even though I couldn't kick my work addiction, I did take two important steps in the right direction during my recovery. The first was finding a church, but not in a building. I had left Catholicism years earlier, but I needed something spiritual, a sense of connection to the world around me and to a greater good. I found that on the top of a hill in my backyard, with Lola and Milo at my side.

I had recently adopted my brother and sister-in-law's Australian shepherd, Milo, a never-ending source of playfulness wrapped up in an athletic, three-year-old body. He never met a living creature he didn't love. With Milo joining our pack in the vineyard paradise, Lola and I finally had our third musketeer.

Mornings were the best. I've always been a morning person, even when I was younger. Waking up to Lola and Milo in my king-sized bed (a real luxury to me that I scored from a friend) was a little like Jenga meets Twister meets a construction zone. It was pure bliss. There was all sorts of non-invasive body contact, elbows crossing legs, tails wagging obtrusively, and just enough gravelly sand deposited on the sheets to remind me that I hadn't checked into a Ritz Carlton.

Our daily morning walks up the hill became our sacred time, our church. We had found each other and had freedom to roam; for that piece of time, we had not a care in the world. There was always at least a slight chill in the air at six in the morning. Even in the dead of summer, with its proximity to the Pacific Ocean, Sonoma County's mercury dipped each night. The morning chill created just enough moisture to coat the grasses, refresh the crisp air, and inject a little burst of energy into our ten legs as we traipsed up the hill. Lola bounded, strong and graceful as a cheetah. Milo, the skilled cattle dog, attempted to herd Lola as well as to encourage me to get moving as my leg dragged us a few clicks slower than their natural pace. But they didn't seem to mind. Eventually, their playful jousting would pave the way to a full-on sprint between the two dear pals. Their faux growls and barks were the only noises cutting into the morning silence. I could find peace in the solitude of nature, and in their welcome intrusions. Their energy was contagious. I was always amazed at how hard they could run. Their joy matched that of top athletes in great competition.

The slope of our hill would gradually give way to a stunning vista of vineyards and valley. The dust kicked up by their energy collected in a small cloud while they patiently waited for me to catch up and see the sun greet us. When I arrived at the top of the hill to watch the sun rise over the majestic landscape, there was an incredible sense of peace, connection, and accomplishment in something inherently good and pure. I could feel spiritual on that hilltop. I could harness hope. I could allow myself the time to focus on the gratitude I had for the land, the beautiful sunrise, the peace, the friendship of Milo and Lola, and for my ability to walk up that hill. I was able to take that time to just appreciate life. This was a big step in the right direction for me. I realize now that I should have done this kind of thing more often.

The second step I took during recovery was finding a human to share our life with. One day at Market, Nick walked back into the kitchen and let me know that Lael was in the dining room and wanted to say hi and see how I was.

Lael. Cute Lael. *Beautiful* Lael. I met her at Jardinière when she was dating Traci's FOH man, Doug Washington. Lael's smile exuded more than just friendly warmth; it always spoke a great kindness to me. When Lael smiled, I felt connected to her calm. A kind of comfort washed over me in her presence. I think the source of her beauty is in her peacefulness and in how clearly genuine she is. But she's also physically beautiful. Her long, dark brown hair gently frames her soft features and smooth skin. She likes to claim that Spanish heritage gave her a rich hue. I think she's colorblind and lying about the Spanish heritage, but her skin *is* gorgeous to this pasty Irish guy.

The last time I had seen Lael, she had asked me out, or so I thought.

"We should get together sometime, catch a movie or a drink," she had said.

She gave me her land line and cell numbers (it was *that* long ago) and told me to call.

I did call. Right away. Both numbers. I had left messages. But no response came. Nothing. I thought maybe I should get my hearing checked. I mean, she had asked me to call. But I was a busy man. So, I moved on.

At Market that day, Nick urged me to go talk with her. "She would love to see you if you can sneak out."

Shit, I thought. *I called her, she blew me off, and then I had brain surgery. Talk about leverage! This will be fun. Hell, yes, I'm going out to the dining room.*

There she was, greeting me with the same calming smile and the same beautiful, but not Spanish, skin. In that moment, like every other moment, she looked lovely and disarming. We caught up. I had a decent amount to fill her in on. She showed sincere interest in my recovery. It was nice. I thought I might even send her some butterscotch pudding when I got back to the kitchen. And eventually, I did have to get back to the kitchen.

"We should get together sometime, grab a drink or a movie," I heard as I stood to make my way back to the kitchen.

Damn, I thought. *Dr. Berger said he got all of the tumor out, but I'm having serious déjà vu. No way they will let me drive a car soon. Shit. Or, am I being punked?*

I stood there for an awkward second, poker faced.

"Here are *my* numbers," I responded with a smile, as I pulled the black sharpie out of my chef jacket pocket and wrote on some gnarly oil and chocolate-tinged piece of scrap paper hibernating in my black chef pants.

The very next day, I listened to my voicemail on my answering machine (it was 2004 when we still had answering machines). Lael's voice played through the speaker.

"Fuck me," I told Cynthia, my roommate, coworker, and Drew's soon-to-be wife. "Should I call her?"

"Not today," Cynthia replied. She was privy to the whole embarrassing story.

I agreed with her thinking. I mean, I had seen the movie *Swingers*. I understood.

I waited three days to return her call. What can I say? I'm Irish; we hold grudges.

She didn't ghost me this time. We went out, and it stuck.

I'm tough to live with. I'm moody, tired, headstrong, often depressed, and I already mentioned the unpleasantness that comes with twelve-to-fourteen-hour days inside a hot, chaotic kitchen. But somehow, Lael's loving calm has kept me grounded and has kept our ever-growing rescue farm of misfits safe and fun. I never got a solid answer as to why she ghosted me the first time. I'm just glad she came back in to check on me. I'm not entirely sure I'd be here today if she hadn't. I was serious about my fear of ending up like Bourdain and Bernard Loiseau. The peace that Lael has given me right along with her love have been instrumental in saving me and in redirecting me to the path I'm on today where I can be a force for positive change and good in the industry I love. Yes, I'm certain that Lael guided me here. Hey, Beautiful, thank you.

CHAPTER TWENTY

"FourFiveSeconds"
by Rihanna, Kanye West, and Paul McCartney

With my professional dream team of Nick and Drew rounded out by my brilliant choice of a life partner in Lael, I had finally positioned myself to launch my four-star dream. The brain tumor was behind me, and Market was running smoothly under Chef Eduardo Martinez's guidance. We were now on a high-speed rail line to open Cyrus. The lease had been signed, and we were in construction, close to opening. But somehow, seemingly out of nowhere, the dream was in serious peril, along with our livelihoods; we had everything invested in that restaurant.

The battle with our once friendly landlord and cohabitant of the building, novice hotel operator David Mars, had turned pretty ugly. When we signed the lease, David had promised us well over $500,000 in TI money, or tenant improvement money, and that we would not have to raise any outside money. In the culinary world, sometimes landlords give restaurant owners money to help them build the space out as it helps improve the value of the landlord's building. TI money entices good talent to enter into a lease. Unfortunately, David couldn't follow through on either of those two promises. He had refused to hire a general contractor for the project. David's mismanagement of the renovations led to several repetitions of building and then tearing down and then building again. Then, he couldn't obtain the permits he needed to finish the hotel and open.

Short in stature, David would march into the restaurant with his slick-back hair, bringing with him a strong aroma of hard alcohol. With pasty, flaky skin, thin, dry lips, and tinted glasses, he threatened to tear up our lease because he thought that we wouldn't be able to hold up our end of the deal and open on time without his funding. I believe he needed us to fail so that we could be his scapegoat for the delay in the hotel opening and budget overruns. If I was older or more experienced, I would have lawyered up much earlier than I did – lesson learned.

"We'll open on time," Nick responded defiantly. "And, what about that TI money?"

"Oh, that money?" David asked. "It's all gone."

David told Nick and me that he had serious doubts that we could pull off the opening of the restaurant without his money. He didn't do his research on us. He didn't know about our work ethic and determination. He didn't imagine that we would actually pound the pavement, raise the money ourselves, and open the restaurant on our own by the time stated on our lease. We also pushed our general contractor, Karl Hasz, to make some magic happen. And Karl came through, big time. Karl got the restaurant done and saved our asses. It was reasonable for David to suspect that we couldn't open without his promised funding. But again, we had the luck of the Irish on our side, Karl, and a Midwest work ethic. We were unstoppable.

On a slightly cold February night our feud erupted. The rain was drizzling at a steady pace. We had just completed one of our first mock services with our newly hired and almost trained Cyrus crew. It was in David's face now that we were really going to open on time, and it boiled his blood.

David was in serious trouble at that point because he couldn't get the certificate of occupancy for the entire building. He couldn't get his lobby tiled or his pool fenced either. Our restaurant and kitchen, on the other hand, were ready to go. Claims that we were holding him up were shot to shit. Moreover, we could collect damages for every day we lost revenue because he was preventing us from opening per the lease requirements.

David returned just in time to see our first test dinner ending. He chose Nick for his target. David called Nick outside in the pouring rain near his unfinished foam façade and began to berate him. When our staff saw the spectacle unfolding, they ran to get me into the kitchen. Nick isn't a fighter at all, which is what makes him the greatest FOH person ever. I, on the other hand, have always been ready to brawl with a bully. I do not relish confrontation, but if someone is out of line, then I'm all in, especially when that bully is picking on a friend. Nick didn't deserve to be spoken to the way that David was speaking to him that night.

I walked straight out into the rain where David was standing. He had backed Nick into the corner of the building that was sheltered from the rain. I got Nick's logic. *Why get wet and cold while I endure this guy's bullshit?* By remaining uncovered in the rain, I assumed David was trying to show how tough he was.

As rain pelted David's head and ran down over his enraged features, he screamed in messy slurs, "I'll ruin you!"

Okay tough guy. I jumped in, stepping between David and Nick. I forced David back out farther into the rain, so that we were both standing in the downpour. My face was just inches from David's, I shouted to match his volume. "You will NEVER speak to Nick like that again."

Our staff scurried around by the door, trying to hear. They were afraid of what they were seeing. This was their livelihood, too.

"We are DONE being pushed around by you," I said as rain pelted my face so that when I had said "pushed," I inadvertently redirected a bit of that rain in a spit onto David. "We raised our own money. We delivered everything we promised, and we're ready to open."

"You'll be hearing from my attorney," David spat back. "I'll DESTROY you."

David's agitation signaled to me that I was dealing with someone unreasonable. There would be no resolution that night. I just needed to end his tirade.

"We can fight it out in court later," I said, my face red with anger and my right leg locked up, a common post-tumor occurrence for me in stressful situations. "But we *are* opening, David. And the clock is running on our expenses. And, by the way, you still owe us that TI money, and we're coming for it."

"You won't open," David slurred. "You can't open without me!"

I wanted him to hit me. At the time, I relished the thought that if I let him hit me a few times, it would increase his legal pain down the road. But now, looking back, I hear the voice inside me warning me that, had he thrown a punch, I would have uncorked on him and not stopped. The restaurant opening was everything to me, and that barely functioning, limp excuse for a man was not going to take it away without a fight.

"We *will* open, David," I seethed, my hair and T-shirt soaked. "Now, grow a sack and finish your building!"

Please just hit me.

Out of the blue, David's son-in-law, who I dubbed Jethro, appeared. He was very obedient to his Daddy Warbucks most of the time. But that night, he stepped in, grabbed David, and walked him away from the scene quickly. That's how it ended that night.

The next four years was jam-packed with one lawsuit after another. David was hell-bent on getting rid of us. It seemed clear to me that he couldn't fathom that this snot-nosed chef would stand up to him and disrespect him.

I had dug in as well. In my mind, we had crossed that line from being able to coexist to being full-on enemies. I had Irish Alzheimer's—forgot everything but the grudges. By then, I was backed by a fully built-out space, and my culinary leverage was growing by the day. I had evened out the playing field originally thrown off balance by David Mars's millions.

We opened Cyrus on March 4, 2005 (03-04-05). But the dream opening was tarnished with the frustrations of having to deal with him and the knowledge, though we weren't ready to admit it yet at that point, that we wouldn't likely be able to function out of that space forever. I had thought that once I opened my own restaurant, I wouldn't have to deal with bullies anymore. This experience was a harsh wake-up call. I realized that I might never be truly free from them.

CHAPTER TWENTY-ONE

"Rockstar"
by Nickelback

Upon opening Cyrus, my only goal in life was to get four stars from the *San Francisco Chronicle* restaurant reviewer, Michael Bauer. Wow, that seems so pathetic to write at this moment. But back then, those stars from Bauer were as necessary as oxygen to me. Ever since reaching the pinnacle at Lespinasse, I was laser focused and probably obsessed. In 2005, the *San Francisco Chronicle* restaurant review mattered more than anything for the future success of the restaurant. Nail it from the start, and it was the gift that would keep on giving. We orchestrated everything we did at Cyrus with that review in the forefront of our minds at every stage—when we were raising money, building the restaurant, planning the menu, and even fighting it out on the rainy sidewalk with David Mars.

Nick and Drew shared my goals. I can't vouch for whether or not their obsession was as strong as mine, but I can say that they more than pulled their weight in the pursuit of the goal. Our entire team did. We knew what was necessary for the success we craved. When the gatekeepers (big-named restaurant reviewers) speak with their pens, the rest of the food world falls in line and pays attention.

The policy at the *Chronicle* was that a restaurant had to be open thirty days before Bauer would begin his judgment; we had thirty days to get our shit together. It was tough, but fair. The other policy was to never award four stars to a restaurant before it was one year old. Thus, a four-star review was not even possible during the first review. Still, I thought he might change it for us. The arrogance of that makes me laugh now. *Did I mention that I was likely obsessed?* Bauer also had a duty to his readers and to his bosses to review new restaurants as quickly as possible. So, we knew that it was not only likely, but probable, that Bauer would pay us a visit exactly thirty-one or thirty-two days after opening. Bauer would come three times at a minimum, usually within day thirty-one to day ninety (intelligence gained from many years of research). This knowledge resulted in about forty-five to sixty days of absolute intensity and never letting up one bit.

We had the same intelligence that the rest of the Bay area chefs and general managers had on Bauer and his life partner, Michael Murphy ("The Michaels"). The intel had been collected and shared over the last twenty plus years that Bauer had been the critic at the *Chronicle*. An actual document kept making the rounds at the high-end restaurants of San Francisco that included a list of the aliases Bauer used to make reservations, phone numbers he had used at previous restaurants to hold reservations, and his car make and model complete with license plate numbers. Those were the Panama Papers of the restaurant business.

But, in reality, once Bauer stepped in the restaurant, we had to perform. I know some chefs were willing to gamble and buy better ingredients on a day they thought he was coming. Wow! Good on their gambling cojones if it paid off for them. But it just seemed easier to me to put our best food forward every day.

The Michaels arrived on the thirty-first day after opening, right on schedule. We had recognized the phone number from our Panama Papers document, but we also knew that he was either coming in on that day or the very next. We were ready. We did not recognize Bauer the other two times he visited, but we were operating on such an intense level that we were ready regardless. The only surprise he could have thrown at us was the time he showed up.

To be clear, I have a rule in my restaurants that my staff and I should never treat one table differently than any other. There are no VIPs in my restaurants. There are friends who might get extra free stuff, but no one gets a better fish or a better steak—though I admit that I gave Jacques Pepin a bigger piece of foie gras terrine once. No one gets pushed ahead of another ticket because of fame or clout. I just don't do it. I saw it way too often in almost every other restaurant I had worked in. VIP meant better treatment, and it bothered me. Everyone was spending the same money. Everyone was a VIP to his or her dining companions. Most importantly, everyone had given me the honor of choosing my restaurant. To me, that equates to equal treatment all the way. I think that my philosophy was refreshing for the cooks and hard for the waiters, but my team worked by my no-VIPs standard.

All that being said, when Bauer walked in, my survival instinct kicked in and usurped all of these values above.

We tried to speed up the other tables so that we could have absolute attention on his table. We couldn't really do anything differently. Our rushing was more to give us time to fix a mistake if we needed it. The Michaels' meals needed to be perfect at all costs. So, a few other tables were likely either pushed along or stalled depending on the almighty Bauer's timing. There was so much riding on that review. It would have been shooting myself in the foot to not buy some insurance. So, we padded the time for Bauer's food. Then, we cooked three of everything his table ordered – more insurance. Although we rarely messed up dishes, when we did mess up a dish we threw it straight into the trashcan. That caused some stress and timing issues. So, instead of reacting to a slightly medium instead of medium-rare piece of meat (it would take twenty minutes to get a new one ready and rested), we just cooked three of the requested dishes to ensure that we'd be able to plate one perfect dish. Later that night, we ate well with all of the leftovers.

One of the subtle things I admired at Lespinasse was that Chef Kunz never came back and cooked for the critics. He let us do it. It made perfect sense. It was my station, and I should be the best at it in the whole kitchen. He tasted the food and would not hesitate to refire anything. But that statement about letting someone do their job was uplifting to me as a cook, and I wanted to pass it on. So, I stayed at the pass (where food passes from the cooks to the guests under the watchful eye and palate of the chef, usually the chef will stand in this area and oversee) except probably a few back and forths to squeeze a meat for temp or to taste sauces.

After Bauer's third visit, we had to wait. Would he come again, or would he call to fact check and ask about specific ingredients and other food details? He had, in the past, called to fact check and then would show up the same day with the *Chronicle's* photographer, throwing a restaurant off balance. Chefs usually assume that after the photographs have been taken, the review is complete, and the staff can take a breather. Not so with that guy.

The review seemed to take forever to come out. It was due out on Sunday. If I waited until very early Saturday morning, I could get the Sunday supplement at the newsstand; we chefs had all done it before. The *Chronicle* had long since been posting content on their website. So I decided to do some sleuthing to see if I could find the review before it appeared in the physical newspaper. I typed *Cyrus* and it popped up. I nearly had a heart attack. I was in the office next to Nick and slapped him. There it was. *Holy shit.* I got nervous. It was all real at that moment. The verdict of everything we had all worked so hard for had arrived on my computer monitor. What was my judgment? Was I any good?

I had read a lot of Bauer's reviews, and I had learned about his dislikes and his attention to details. I knew what was important to him. I ate at the places Bauer wrote about to gain a better understanding of how the man worked. I also respected Bauer's palate—a lot. He understood flavors quite well. I'm sure my opinion of Bauer's review was and is skewed because the content was of such great importance to me, but what I read in that review was inspired writing. And, *holy shit*, it was about me, about Cyrus, about our dream, and about our future. He got everything I was trying to do. He labeled me as "now in the pantheon of four-star chefs."

Bauer wrote, "Keane's star has been launched, and Sonoma now has its next superstar chef."

Bauer understood my seasonings, sauces, acid, and the push and pull. *Holy shit. I could cook!* We did not get four stars that day. Policy is policy, even stupid policy. But Bauer wrote the Cyrus review as a four-star review. He even wrote that it was "amazing" how quickly we were operating on that high of a level so soon after opening. One year later, when we were technically eligible, Bauer did come back and make our four stars official.

When I finished reading that first review, I was instantly nauseous and freaked out. I wanted that review more than anything; but somehow, I wasn't ready for those words. I knew that along with that review, there would be greater expectations from our dining guests. It's a weird thing. A great food critic can and should be able to pick up on things that a normal guest can't, like subtlety, ingredient nuance, and personality in cooking. A typical guest, on the other hand, knows what he or she likes. If the food deviates from that typical guest's preferences or comfort level, then it's a turn off. Also, some restaurant frequenters read reviews like Bauer's and immediately want to prove that they know better. They come looking for faults.

"*I*," insert pretentious tone, "eat at *all* the best restaurants, and I'll have you know that *this* isn't . . ."

Thus, the moment my dream was realized, a pit in my stomach warned me about the hurricane on the horizon of the sleepy town of Healdsburg. We had been launched into the stratosphere of elite, fine dining with all its powerful magnifying glasses. My life as I knew it was about to change forever, and not all for the better.

CHAPTER TWENTY-TWO

"Royals"
by Lourde

Michael Bauer and the *San Francisco Chronicle* were very important and powerful gatekeepers, but there are plenty of other critics and stars to be awarded out there. It feels like there is no end to this industry's ability to tout another critic's award to perpetuate hype in the press. And we chefs crave and go after the stars, reviews, and awards exactly like drug addicts needing a fix. Once we get three stars, we want four. When we get four stars, we seek the next critic's stars. When we get that critic's affirmations, we immediately need another fix. More, more, more!

To complicate matters, and make us restaurant folk scramble a bit more, different critics use different scales to judge us. My local newspapers, *San Francisco Chronicle* and the Sonoma County newspaper, *The Press Democrat*, judged on a scale of four stars. Beyond our local publications, Mobil (yeah, the gasoline company) and AAA (yes, the travel insurance company) use a five-star rating system. Zagat started using a point system rather than stars, but then switched to a five-star scale over time, whereas Gayot Publications has stuck with its twenty-point scale system. San Pellegrino (indeed, the water company) publishes "The World's 50 Best" and "The World's 100 Best," yielding two days of press releases to the lucky top fifty. So, when someone mentions five-star or four-star quality, it should be put into context.

I promise you that the chefs and general managers of the restaurants and hotels study each and every point and star and try to discern how to get them. Some of the guides are more willing to share their criterion than others. This seems fair to me. Tell us what you are judging us on so that we can choose to compete if we want. It evens the playing field and helps keep a check on the critics' power.

So, to recap, the masters of a restaurant's destiny up until 2007 included a water company, a gas company, an insurance company, and newspapers . . . *oh my!* It was almost a municipality in its own right. But in San Francisco in 2006, there wasn't yet a tire company telling people where to eat. Thus, in 2007, the fine French people of Michelin decided to venture into the Bay Area to grace us with their veiled opinion on which chefs were good enough. With one simple announcement, Michelin turned the entire chef population of the San Francisco Bay area into silly putty. There was a new sheriff in town.

Chefs are acutely aware of the Michelin-starred restaurants in France. They are the epitome of high-end gastronomy, with three stars being reserved for only the best of the best. The Michelin rating system is defined, on their website, as follows: One Star— "A very good restaurant;" Two Stars— "Excellent cooking that is worth a detour;" and Three Stars— "Exceptional cuisine that is worth a special journey."

Michelin's arrival in San Francisco really did change the game. Instead of sitting in a circle jerk and discussing whether four stars from *The New York Times* was as good as four stars from the *San Francisco Chronicle*, or whether five stars from Mobil was equal to a spot on the "Top 50 Best," or even if a twenty on Gayot was the equivalent of a thirty on Zagat, we discussed Michelin and Michelin alone. We believed that Michelin would somehow give us a definitive worldwide standard of excellence.

Michelin, a French owned and operated worldwide tire company, had started off rating restaurants as a way to help people find a good place to eat as they traveled across the countryside of France. But this simple premise quickly evolved into a way to encourage traveling to the highly rated restaurants. And guess what? More driving equates to more tire sales. So, this tire company, run by marketing geniuses, ended up as the most revered restaurant critic around the world. Michelin's motive remains to sell more tires, not simply to find the best food in the world. Might they find some good restaurants? Sure. But it's critical to understand that Michelin is not a member of the restaurant industry, nor do its mysterious critics provide a resumé to prove that they have culinary industry experience. Still, Michelin rose above all other restaurant critics and expanded around the globe. And here's the kicker; no one is versed in the specific criteria Michelin uses to judge, if it even exists.

Surely, I thought at the time, *they must have a meticulous system of grading restaurants.* I mean, the marketing machine of *The Michelin Guide* is flawless. They established themselves for many years as experts. They have a responsibility to be above reproach with so much power, right? One Michelin star could book a restaurant for months, if not years. The loss of a star? Well, the mere thought caused Chef Bernard Loiseau to take his life rather than risk the appearance of failure in the eyes of the almighty Michelin inspectors.

Let me break this down for you further. First, Michelin's critics are anonymous. We are told that these critics go through a rigorous training process in order to be the final say, but we don't know what that training entails. Second, Michelin's judging criteria is so vague that it's impossible to know how to prepare for a Michelin critique. According to its website, there are five criteria:

1. Quality of the products
2. Mastery of flavor and cooking techniques
3. The personality of the chef in his cuisine
4. Harmony of the flavors
5. Consistency between inspectors' visits

Michelin also posts that the core values of their critics are *anonymity, independence, expertise, reliability, passion, and quality*—pretty much just a bunch of words thrown on paper to create an air of superiority and integrity. But when you break it down, there's nothing concrete in these criteria at all. *How convenient.*

Even though I've grown very weary of being judged by people who have never walked in my shoes, I don't actually begrudge any of the ratings systems or critics their right to make a living and sell some travel guides or newspapers. It just needs to be said that they make their bucks off the backs of people who are barely scraping by and doing a really tough job. Restaurant workers like cooks, dishwashers, and waiters struggle to pay rent and health insurance. The word of a critic has real-life consequences for restaurant workers. So, it's unsettling that a tire company has so much sway over the lives of these industrious people when we don't even know how the Michelin critics are trained to critique. Moreover, Michelin doesn't provide feedback to restaurants seeking to improve. By contrast, Mobil sends a restaurant a report filled out by its inspectors. *San Francisco Chronicle* critic Michael Bauer would in his reports own *why* he thought your tuna tartar sucked. He couldn't just strip a restaurant down from four to three stars without clearly communicated justification. Michelin justifies nothing.

To sum it up, we have no idea who Michelin hires to be its critics or what qualifications those critics have. We don't know how those mysterious Michelin critics judge restaurants. We don't know how to improve if given a bad review from Michelin. And Michelin never justifies any rating they give. It boggles the mind that we have bought into this. In 2007, the mere mention of Michelin in San Francisco elicited a response of "I'm not worthy" along with a mutter of "but a star would be nice."

There is a cultural component to Michelin's power that should be noted. In Europe, one star is something that careers are made of. Three stars is unheard of. In America, one star out of three is considered a failure.

"They only got *one* star? *Jesus.*"

And, if Forbes or Mobil rates my restaurant at five out of five stars, and Michelin rates me at two out of three stars, then which is better or right? Which has any real meaning at all?

After Cyrus received two Michelin stars, I had to pull my nose out of Le French ass. I decided to switch two of my four tires on my F150 truck. Had I gotten three stars, I might have switched all four. But I had some pride left. Yes, business increased considerably. The press and exposure were enormous, and, like the drug Dilaudid when I was in the hospital, I wanted another dose. Two Michelin Stars was my Dilaudid. The rush of figuring out how to get the third star (an impossible task, remember) became my new mission in life. I put myself on the same trajectory as Bernard Loiseau, and I think that deep down, I knew how dangerous the path was even before Bernard took his own life.

In his book "The Perfectionist: Life & Death in Haute Cuisine" Rudolph Chelminski writes that when Bernard finally received the call that he was being awarded his third Michelin star, the penultimate achievement for his culinary crusade, he immediately sat down to a celebratory lunch and pondered out loud to his dining companions, "I wonder if Michelin would ever award a fourth star?" A few years later, when he heard a rumor that Michelin was going to take away a star, Bernard committed suicide. The cruel rumor was false, by the way. Bernard didn't lose a star, but his wife and daughter lost him.

I can relate to Bernard, and it scares the hell out of me. I wasn't happy with just two stars; I wanted three. *But Daddy I want an Oompa Loompa now!* Unlike Veruca Salt, I was willing to work for it. I was willing to do anything for it.

Is our bread good enough? Let's build a half-million-dollar bakery kitchen, staff it all day, make eight-to-ten perfect mini breads, and give them away for free to our guests. Not enough? Let's close for two days a week so I can be here for every service. Let's update our china, glass, and silverware to the tune of a hundred grand. Let's do whatever we have to do so I can get that third star.

I needed affirmation and to protect my partners and employees. Let me be very clear about this; if I had ever lost a Michelin star, Cyrus would have tanked, bills would not have been paid, and jobs would have been lost. The livelihood of every person working at Cyrus and their families was at stake. So, I know Bernard's despair well.

Every year, when it was time for Michelin to do their annual announcement of stars awarded, chefs would get a cryptic email a few weeks before stating that "the director would like to speak with you." Then, the chefs have to wait to hear if they gained or lost a star. I grew more than disenchanted by the fifth year waiting for my phone to ring. I felt like a snot-nosed eighth grader hoping to get invited to the Sadie Hawkins dance.

When the phone finally rang that day, I boldly asked the woman on the other end, "What's your name?"

She stumbled and replied with a giggle, "I can't tell you that."

"Well," I replied, "then what are you wearing?"

Lael, listening in very close by, almost spit up her chilly glass of sauvignon blanc when she heard my tone.

I wanted to communicate to the Michelin critic some of the absurdity that existed in this relationship. *Seriously, make up a fucking name for the call, lady.* The cloak-and-dagger routine was wearing thin.

As the media hype increased after my stars were awarded, I noticed a change in myself and my staff. When I peeked out of my glass doors during service, I no longer saw as many happy faces and engaged diners conversing with each other as I had in previous years. Those happy faces had brought me utter delight and fueled my passion for my craft. But after Michelin came on the scene, many others followed suit to critique Cyrus. Then, instead of only joy in my dining room, I saw a lot of muted white light emanating from the little glass and plastic extensions of guests' hands while they snapped pictures and typed furiously on their phones to meet some self-imposed customer-rating app deadline. It was like a bunch of water had been thrown on the Bauer and Michelin inspector gremlins; the judges had multiplied, and the result was disastrous.

I should explain that I believe that every guest in any of my restaurants is absolutely entitled to their opinions about whether or not they like my food. That opinion is based on a guest's palate and preferences. I have nothing against a guest expressing that opinion. The problem arises, as I see it, when an unqualified guest attempts to give a technical critique about whether the food was prepared properly. A dish can be prepared with technical perfection, and a guest might just not care for it; but that doesn't mean that the chefs messed up. That's the difference—cooking technique as opposed to personal preferences, and the inability of many people to thread that needle successfully. In addition, by paying so much attention to writing reviews, diners lose the simple pleasure of the dining experience—enjoying good food with friends and family.

Would my dining guests ever again be able to simply enjoy a meal without checking their phones or documenting the experience? Would I ever be able to really divorce myself from the critics, or would I end up like Loiseau?

CHAPTER TWENTY-THREE

"Back in Black"
by AC/DC

The first time Michelin unleashed their power and fury on the Bay Area, the press took the bait; the Michelin marketing machine knew what it was doing. A steady stream of articles built tension, speculation, and excitement for a full year before the actual stars were announced. Reading about Michelin became entertainment. And Cyrus was in the middle of it. When Cyrus was awarded two stars, I got more culinary leverage than ever. I didn't realize it right away, but it didn't take very long.

The announcement was made at the Michelin Gala, where we all paraded in like peacocks to accept our gifts while lightbulbs from photographers popped simultaneously with the champagne. The next morning, Nick and I had to attend our mediation with David Mars. The battle had been going on for more than three years at that point, and the judge pushed us to try mediating rather than go to trial.

With a slight hangover from the free bubbles and very little sleep, Nick and I arrived at the nondescript strip mall building in Santa Rosa at eight-thirty with our attorneys, Barbara, and my brother Chris; our expectations were low.

I had planned on just sitting back and letting the mediators and the lawyers have the floor. But that all changed the moment the mediator walked into the room with the newspaper.

Pointing to my picture from the gala on the front page, the mediator asked with a big grin, "How does it feel to be the most famous person in Sonoma County?"

The question took me back for a second. *Was he buttering me up?* I deflected politely and offered that we were honored and surprised. That's when it clicked. Although Michelin and Bauer had given me the leverage, the mediator's comment made me realize that the power I had could be used in the mediation even if it did originate in a kitchen. In that moment, I knew that all of David Mars's millions had just been neutralized by the mediator's one comment.

Over the next sixteen hours (yeah, we stayed until one in the morning), I put on a show that flexed every ounce of my new power into a settlement that was simply not possible until that day. I was able to end that Hatfield and McCoy feud in our favor. And I was just getting started with exercising my new-found influence.

In the next few years, my celebrity increased through a series of TV appearances and articles in print and online. Something inside of me urged me to use my leverage for good, and I felt a strong desire to find a way to help shelter dogs. I think that the director of the Healdsburg Animal Shelter (HAS) thought I was joking when I first called over and asked if I could volunteer. Somehow, in the middle of my twelve-hour days at Cyrus, I had found enough energy to take an online dog training course. In order to receive the certification I wanted, I needed to volunteer at a shelter. Lael and I had always dreamed of turning our five-acre property into an animal sanctuary with a focus on abandoned or injured dogs. So, I figured I'd get my dog trainer certification and get started in my hometown at our shelter. I also liked that HAS had branded itself as a no-kill shelter, which led me to believe that all animals got to stay alive.

I believe the director saw dollar signs when I convinced her that I really did want to volunteer. My ability to help fundraise increased every time I earned a new accolade. I was willing to leverage my celebrity in that way. Anything for pups.

My first day at HAS, I was teamed up with Valerie, a volunteer trainer adviser who specialized in the tougher cases. These were dogs that needed a little more time before they could be deemed adoptable. Valerie's passion lay in transforming the scared and nonsocial pups into loving family members that could find a forever home; right up my alley. That day, a new dog needed an evaluation.

Valerie and I walked back to where the new doggie refugee named Cash was being housed in his new cell called a kennel. *Dear God, he's big*, I thought. The size of a dirt bike at over a hundred pounds, this brindle-colored behemoth mix of Catahoula Leopard Dog, Great Dane, mastiff and pittie looked more like a Bengal tiger with a Cro-Magnon skull than a canine. The fact that this creature was shaking with fear in his new, cold, steel home terrified me and broke my heart at the same time. The poor pup was shaking and crying. This stunningly handsome beast was both scary and sad. Had it not been for Valerie's presence and guidance, I don't think I would have been able to go any further. I'm so glad she was there.

Valerie announced that she was going in, and I was sincerely baffled. No way was I going in. I needed my hands to cook. But what would I do if Cash ate her? Valerie sauntered into his cage. Cash's response was curious to me. He didn't lunge. Instead, he simply lay down, ears back, and looked in my direction. I moved just a bit closer to the cage as Valerie tried to get acquainted with Cash. He looked again in my direction. *He's looking at the goddamn noose they used to drag him in there!* I immediately grabbed the noose and moved it out of sight. Cash's entire body released immediately. Then, his smile emerged, and he started to cozy up to Valerie even though he was still whining and whimpering a little.

"Hmm, maybe he needs to go to the bathroom?" Valerie asked out loud.

At the sound of the word *bathroom*, Cash immediately jumped up.

We scrambled to get a leash on him as we finally realized the urgency of the situation. We ran him to the nearest patch of grass, and the poor guy pissed for four minutes straight. He had been trained not to go inside by a family he loved and would be obedient to even after they had abandoned him. His gratitude to us upon being relieved was immediately evident. Cash no longer looked scary. He was just a playful dog in need of a friend and a home.

I immediately fell in love with this gentle giant even with his massive forehead and jaw that could swallow a small turkey. Most of the other volunteers were afraid of him because of his appearance. To be fair, his size and strength made it impossible for some of the volunteers to walk him. There really were only two of us who could take him out. So, for the next few months, I would run over from Cyrus and make sure he got out three times a day so that he wouldn't have to compromise his principles and soil his cell.

Cash and I became pretty close. He even showed me that he already knew some tricks—lie down, roll over, shake, hugs, and kisses. I think he was telling me that I was the lucky guy who was going to take him home; I just didn't know it yet. I did want him, but it wasn't in the cards quite yet because Lael's dog was older and not social.

Over the next few months, Cash almost got adopted a few times. But the adoptions fell through for various reasons. He was getting depressed in his prison cell, and I was getting worried. I had seen too many animals at HAS euthanized. I had believed HAS was a no-kill shelter—until then. I learned that *no-kill* is a term of art used by animal shelter marketers that originated from noble intentions. The label is used to entice shelters that killed high percentages of dogs to kill fewer of them. No-kill technically means that the shelter cannot kill more than 10 percent of the animals in their care. I couldn't deal with seeing so many animals euthanized, even if only one out of ten. Thus, I had to drift away. Rather than voice my opinion, as I was not an expert by any means, I just found another place to donate my time—King's Kastle. But I still kept a close eye on my buddy, Cash.

I was told that the director was pretty upset that I wasn't going to be her golden goose of fundraising. Truth is, I would still have helped out for the dogs. But then, about a month later, word got back to me that Cash's time was up; the director didn't believe he was adoptable; he was too big and scary, and he had developed kennel aggression towards other dogs due to his solitary confinement. Cash was on death row.

The DNA of a chef (ego and all) demands that the chef fix things by muscling through them. If that fails, then we use our brains. I became determined to find a way to make it work with both Lael's dog and Cash at home.

I immediately called HAS and said, "I want to adopt Cash."

"No," was the reply. "He's not up for adoption. *You* can't have him."

I was stunned, but I regrouped. "How about I pay for him to go to Kings Kastle to get rehabbed for his kennel aggression?"

That was something HAS periodically did with so-called *trouble dogs*.

"Nope."

Nope? I started to think that this might be personal.

I called a friend who was both an attorney and an HAS board member. I told him everything. He agreed that the situation didn't sound right and said that he would look into it.

A few hours later, my lawyer friend called me back. "Yeah, the adoption's not going to happen. I'm not sure why, but she's not going to give you that dog."

The hell she isn't, I thought. I was going to use my culinary leverage to save Cash.

"Okay" I said. "It's Wednesday now. If I don't have that dog by Monday, I'm going to sue the shelter. And none of us wants that. I'm not going to let HAS kill him. Fair warning, okay?"

He brushed it off politely because, in my opinion, he was kind of in a hopeless situation. And secondly, I don't think he believed me.

Well, come Monday I delivered on my promise and filed suit. Chefs get shit done. The truth is, I had absolutely zero legal standing. Our legal case was below flimsy according to Rex, my new local lawyer. But I knew I was right, and I was willing to spend whatever leverage I had to save my buddy.

The front-page headline that followed was perfect: *Local Chef Sues Animal Shelter.*

Radio DJs read it. The jury pool read it. *Everyone* in Sonoma read it. Then, the *San Francisco Chronicle* picked it up. It was a compelling story, and I knew it. Legal standing? Blah, blah, blah. Diplomacy? Blah, blah, blah. Pure unadulterated use of my celebrity power? Yep. I would not abandon Cash. He had already been abandoned once before, and I was not going to let that happen to him again. No way.

After about a month of hard-hitting press and an attempt or two to smear me, Cash was handed over to me. He spent a few months at Kings Kastle and then moved home with us. Cash lived out his life along with five other dogs, two pigs, two sheep, three goats, and a few cows. He was beloved by everyone who met him—except my brother. I think it was the Cro-Magnon skull.

"This is the dog?" people asked when meeting him.

"Yep. That's Cash."

Losing him hurt. His large presence and majestic soul have not yet been replaced, but my life was greater having had him as a friend.

The power of that experience showed me that chefs had attained a new level of influence that they simply did not have when I started out in the business. People began to treat me with reverence. The press would cover me on demand. Everything I did seemed interesting to other people. They *fawned* over me. They wanted to get to know me and to spend time with me, all because I could cook a good risotto. It was a little scary. I felt kind of the same, but somehow different. I don't think I knew how different.

Suddenly, I couldn't go to the grocery store without someone peering into my cart with curiosity. I guess the thought was that if they saw me on TV they were entitled to look in my grocery basket? *Yeah, that's toilet paper for my ass.* I've also never gotten used to the way people started to address me as *Chef* outside of my restaurant. These people didn't work with me or for me, so the courtesy title made no sense. It's not the title that makes me uncomfortable; it's more about how they do it and why. In a way, my aversion to being called Chef outside my kitchen stemmed from a feeling that I was losing my identity as Doug. So, I have a request. If you see a chef outside of his restaurant, and you don't work in that chef's restaurant, please don't address her or him as *Chef.* Using someone's first name feels more human to me. I know you might think it's a sign of respect, but we just make dinner.

The other problem with culinary leverage is that it can lead some chefs to abuse their influence. Mario Batali was accused of groping and assaulting women with the delusion that they were into his overweight, sweaty, red Croc and tight short wearing, hard-partying rock star chef persona. Gordon Ramsey's most frequent method of communication became screaming. He regularly screamed at struggling line cooks who had to hold back their defiance for fear of getting kicked off the culinary island in TV land. These kitchen staff workers are real people who are just trying to pay the rent and learn a craft. Terrance Brennan literally chased this young cook out of his kitchen, I can only assume to instill a level of fear in his staff. Think about it, *please*. Please think about it the next time you laugh at the cooking reality show on TV, or you smirk when you hear a *chefs gone wild* story. It's not right that our culture has cheered on these unhealthy workplace environments. How have we allowed this to happen? It's just dinner. Our culture has become so enamored with celebrity that we went looking for a bunch of insecure, affirmation seeking, barely skilled laborers, and we made them into rock stars via TV. If we aren't careful, we might—again—elevate a con man and failed real estate developer/TV personality to the presidency.

Still, there are a lot of chefs doing good things with their leverage because they are good people. Jose´ Andres feeds the hungry during catastrophes, and the Italian Chef Massimo Bottura feeds the homeless. In my neck of the woods, we have chefs like Nancy Oakes of Boulevard fame, who not only spearheads Meals on Wheels, but also almost every other charity that exists. In Sonoma County, I don't think Chef Dustin Valette has ever said no to helping a charitable cause when asked. Both of these local heroes give me constant inspiration when I need to buckle up and put my big boy pants on to help others, instead of sitting on the sidelines. Even though I don't feel my power is deserved, I've got it now, and I'm determined to use it for good.

CHAPTER TWENTY-FOUR

"In Your Eyes" (Live) by Jeffrey Gaines

As my leverage increased with each new award, I learned that it had the ability to take me places. Literally. I suddenly had the opportunity to travel to places I would never have been able to visit had my red wine risotto not been on point when Mr. Bauer or Madame Michelin walked through Cyrus's doors. It took me a while to sift through the ego-based travel and events to figure out what was important to me and how I could make this leverage and hard work fruit for myself, Lael, and my causes.

The restaurant industry preys upon its own lifeblood, the chefs, by creating countless industry events and charity events that can be significant media opportunities leading to more of the almighty exposure. Let's call these events circle jerks. These events demand time out of an already frenetic schedule, but they lure us in when they are held to raise money for great causes. As ego based as chefs are, many of us have a deep reservoir of desire to help people. It just never seems to be anonymous. *Circle* meet *Jerk*. So many of these events are where chefs donate their time and product in order to be included with the cool kids. These food and wine festivals scattered across the globe offer a Venus flytrap setting for everyone except the people making the money. The need to stay relevant and feel included is strong.

For almost ten years, pre and during Cyrus, I attended many events in an effort to chase stature. But the work was wearing me down. In order to work these events, I had to rearrange my schedule, leave my animals, and even Lael, most times, sacrificing what little down time I had. I flew around the country to work my ass off, would fly back home, and go back to work jet lagged and cranky. And for what? Because I wanted to be one of the cool kids? Around 2010, I finally realized that I was sick of working for free. I decided that from then on, minus the charity events that were important to me, that the cost to get me to leave my family and animals would be commensurate with my efforts for the event. I was officially done bartering my back for PR and exposure. Thus, when the marketing woman from Four Seasons Hotel in Bangkok called with a request that I work there for a week, I was ready.

"Really?" she asked when I politely declined her offer.

She was nice, and obviously a good salesperson. But my bluntness threw her off balance.

"Yeah, really. I can go to a beach resort anytime on my own. It's not worth working my butt off in a sweaty hotel kitchen for five nights plus prep all day to go sit on a beach. But thanks."

"Okay, what would it take?" she offered. "We really would like you to come."

That was my moment. It took me fifteen years to be able to make a request like I did in that conversation.

"Well," I replied smoothly, "I love animals, and I know you have an elephant sanctuary in Chiang Rai." The sanctuary was not far from the Bangkok hotel. "I'd like to go there with my wife for three days and play with the elephants."

"*Ohhh.*" She dragged the word out a little, emphasizing her subtle shock. "That's not possible. It's really expensive."

"I understand," I said lightly. "No worries. Thanks, though."

"*Really?* You really aren't going to do it?" she asked in her best plaintiff's wail.

"Nope, not worth it," I shot back with utter confidence, quite proud of myself.

"Let me see what I can do," she grumbled.

And just like that, Lael and I were granted admission to the elephant sanctuary in the Golden Triangle. We were technically in the country of Thailand, but a stone's throw away from Burma and Laos. This is a very storied part of the world that fueled opium trade for hundreds of years. But the violent history is offset by the natural beauty of hills, jungle, and ever-stretching waters. I'm still not sure how the Four Seasons fits into the humane sanctuary business, but my three-day stay left me with the impression that the elephants were loved and cared for. Each elephant had a dedicated mahout who spent his entire life bonding with and caring for his elephant.

My elephant was Yuki. She was beautiful and magnificent, sweet, and smart, and above all, loving. She owned me from the first second we met. I fed her bananas; not four or five, but like fifty at a time. Peel and all. She smiled. With her wrinkled, weathered, beautifully aged skin, her sweet face reminded me of Mother Teresa's. Her massive tongue gently protruded when she opened her enormous mouth to allow me to place her morning bananas directly in. When she lifted her long, powerful trunk to give me access to her mouth, she was revealing her full trust in me to feed her the treats she deserved just for existing in this world. Her enormity was matched only by her calming presence.

Lael and I spent three glorious days at the elephant camp, walking among the animals by day and nestling into a pretty luxurious tent by night. Via good old Stan's relationship with his former employer (Four Seasons), I was given the unusual privilege of bathing Yuki. I sat on top of her and scrubbed her back with a huge, deck-like brush as they hosed her off. I rinsed her head as she slowly knelt fifteen feet down in the "pond," and I nearly fell off. Lael and the mahout standing on dry ground chuckled at my lack of balance. I wouldn't have cared one bit if I had fallen. She could've rolled on top of me and crushed me, and I would have died happy.

I also played with a baby elephant. Though elephants are normally very protective of their newborns, one particularly seasoned mother was a little more freewheeling with her third child. She kept a watchful eye as the two-hundred-plus-pound pup and I wrestled. He grabbed my glasses off my head and wrapped his trunk around me in a slithering, silly love fest. It was like playing with a rambunctious lab puppy, but bigger. Because this baby elephant was the only young elephant around, he was starved for some playtime. I was more than willing to fill in his mosh pit. We both laughed so hard as we giggled and wrestled that I cried. That experience made my work trip more than worth it. I had used my culinary leverage to push away from the Fantasy Island beach vacation to instead connect with those enchanting creatures. Joy matters.

On the final morning, I asked if I could skip my breakfast and take my time to say goodbye to Yuki. We walked through the mud and rain to see her and bring her treats. An overwhelming sadness overcame me. I loved her, and I knew I would never see her again. Every time Yuki had gazed into my eyes, she had shown me her soul. I stood next to her that last morning gently stroking her ear and talking to her mahout. Yuki nudged me a little in a playful, but strong way. I didn't respond. Ten seconds later, she leaned in a little more with her craggy ears and rubbed her trunk against the drying mud on my neck. I looked at the mahout and asked if she was asking for more food.

He smiled. "No. She knows you. She's saying goodbye."

With tears, I kissed Yuki's ear and told her that I loved her. I realized then that the leverage I'd acquired really could be used to help me attain the more balanced, healthier life I'd promised myself before my brain surgery. More than just a balanced life, this leverage could grant me extraordinary experiences if I let it.

CHAPTER TWENTY-FIVE

"Hook"
by Blues Traveler

One special evening, I had the privilege of traveling to Scottsdale Arizona to cook for one of my heroes, Muhammad Ali. It was a celebrity-studded seventieth birthday celebration for the greatest boxer of all time. A chef friend, Beau MacMillan ("BoMac" for short), included me in the group of chefs for this magical experience. We cooked, but we were treated so well that I truly felt like one of the guests. I admired Ali and his unfailing courage more than I could ever describe. The guests, including Mia Hamm, Lance Armstrong, Tony Hawk, and Dusty Baker came to dine with the GOAT; the money went to a variety of Ali's charities.

Although age had stripped Ali's boxer agility, the man clearly embraced the energy of the crowd that night in the large, packed banquet hall. He joyfully greeted every person in that room as they approached to pay their respects to the living hero. During the meal, the famous athletes in the room each had a turn to stand and say a few words about what Ali meant to them. I found myself imagining what it must be like for Ali to witness the effect that he had had on so many people. Somehow, while observing this beautiful event, Muhammad Ali became more real to me.

Ali was no longer just a superhero-like figure; he was a real person who had the courage to lead by example and speak up against cultural norms. He had the discipline to do his best every single day. He feared neither his next opponent in the ring, nor the press, nor any possible ramifications of his activism. He stood firm, worked his ass off, and spoke the truth. In that moment, I appreciated him even more. Ali's greatness stemmed from the fact that he used his celebrity to inspire others.

The highlight of the event for me was hearing Major League Baseball great, Dusty Baker, relive a story from his childhood in which he listened to Ali's fight on the radio with his father. Dusty recalled being a young, Black child and personally struggling with his place in our country. After the fight, Baker heard a young Ali take the microphone.

Ali announced to the world through the radio that "I am a beautiful man. I am a dangerous man."

Baker recalled that Ali gave him a much-needed sense of pride and strength. Dusty wanted to be a beautiful and dangerous man, too. And Ali, a hero of heroes, gave him that inspiration. When Dusty stood and spoke from his table, I wasn't the only one captivated. The rest of the room was silent. I was left with a greater appreciation of the magnitude of Ali's inspiration. It was important. One man was *that* important.

When Lael and I returned to our hotel room that night, a gift was waiting—an autographed boxing glove from Muhammad Ali. We both teared up. It was deeply moving to us to have the privilege of spending a bit of time with Ali and with so many others who shared our admiration. The signed glove reminded us of how one person can positively touch the lives of so many others. To this day it reminds me that I must try to use my modicum of celebrity do the same in whatever small ways I can.

CHAPTER TWENTY-SIX

"All For You"
by Sister Hazel

After a few soul-enriching experiences, I was determined to pay it forward in my kitchen and lead by example. I wanted to cook ground-breaking food, and I wanted to do it in a healthy, positive environment. When the faculty of the Kyoto Culinary Academy in Japan invited me to join them for a two-week immersion into the Kaiseki cooking method, I was honored. This was a huge gift to learn more about my craft and expand my understanding of the Japanese flavors that I deeply loved. I knew the experience would elevate my cooking, and I would then be able to bring that knowledge home and share it with my staff.

But an internal conflict arose during my two weeks at the academy. The experience, up until the point of my conflict, had been an absolute delight. Japan is steeped in tradition. Japanese chefs have enormous respect for how things have traditionally been done as well as how they should be done. I was having trouble with one of the traditions; I was asked to kill a turtle.

Besides some trout back in college and a plethora of lobsters, I had never killed anything I cooked. I do realize the complicated and inconvenient irony of being a person who serves animal proteins to people on a daily basis while claiming to be an animal advocate. It seems duplicitous, I know.

That day at the Japanese academy, a turtle appeared out of a box, and my Japanese chef host for that day cast a slightly amused smile my way. I don't think he knew the true depth of the issue at hand. His grin communicated that this was a test he gave all chefs he taught. The turtle, just a bit bigger than my hand stretched out, was placed on the cutting board. The chef glanced at me again. I knew what he was saying. It was time. No translation needed. He offered me his razor-sharp knife and instructed me to grab the turtle's soft neck and pull to expose as much of it as possible.

The super-thin, carbon-steel blade felt surprisingly heavy in my hand. No part of me wanted to do it. *But I'll be too hypocritical if I don't do this*, I thought. Like jumping out of an airplane (which I've also done, by the way), I pushed emotion and thought from my mind, grasped the creature, and slit its throat. It was quick and physically painless from my perspective, but it wasn't my throat. The kill was almost instant.

In the reality of eating and serving living things, this kill seemed humane. But it wasn't something I wanted to do again. I've always known that if I had to sacrifice the animals I ate, I would become a vegetarian. Somehow, I'm able to disassociate the carcasses I butcher and sauté from the animals I pass in the fields. I'm grateful for that coping skill. But I'm also grateful for being placed in that uncomfortable situation in that Kyoto kitchen. It made me think more deeply about the choices I make in terms of what I purchase and how the animals are treated. I'm thankful for the people who humanely as possible do the hunting and the slaughtering. I'm also thankful that I don't have to do it. I'm not the first chef who has struggled with this, I'm sure.

Aside from the turtle incident, this trip was pivotal in my evolution as a chef in both my technical cooking and in my idea of an ideal kitchen environment. Those two still to this day affect how I work and engineer my menus. In Japan, and especially in Kyoto, there are many people who specialize and take great pride in doing one thing their entire life perfectly. My background was very different. I bounced all over the place, learned whatever I could soak up, and then created my spin on what my food would be. That process was much more suited to the way my mind works. But to study with people who had been perfecting their one specific cuisine, a cuisine with which I was obsessed, was somewhat magical.

I inquired as to why they were so generous with their time and money, as I could not see the payback here for the Culinary Academy group of chefs. There was no Japanese product push, and it was not a short-term investment for them. Their answer to my question was enlightening. The elders of the group had realized that, as much as being steeped in their traditions had worked for them, it had also closed them off a little. The rich culture had been somewhat of a creative noose, and they wanted to expose their younger counterpoints to other chefs and to other ways of cooking. They decided to invite four accomplished chefs from different parts of the world every year and immerse them with their chefs. They knew that while the foreign chefs learned from them, they would also learn from the foreign chefs. That was the quid pro quo, an investment on both ends that would pay dividends many times over. With their rough, proud, and extremely generous demeanors, my Japanese counterparts were paying it forward.

I adored their food. The flavors spoke to me, and the use of umami and, in some cases acid, to satiate instead of using fat and carbs was an important lesson. I learned how to create dishes that would allow my guests to experience a fourteen-course meal and walk away feeling light but satisfied. This became a key element in how I would shape my menus.

The most important thing that I took away from my time in Japan was learning the pace and energy of their kitchens. It was remarkably calm and even soothing. There was something about the peaceful kitchens that struck a deep chord with me. The tight, small kitchens served extremely elaborate multi-course meals executed flawlessly. But there was no rush, no hurried pace, and no kinetic sparks like I was so used to. From as far back as I can remember, if I wasn't rushing and stressing about getting the next dish out when working, then I felt like I wasn't working hard enough, or I was doing something wrong. In the kitchens I had worked in, the adrenaline and noise had been as much a part of the culture as the food. It was consistent from Michigan, to New York, to Washington, to San Francisco, and to my kingdom at Cyrus. I realized that I had carried the tradition with me into my own restaurant. I realized that I didn't need to create stress and dark energy to have intensity and perfection. In fact, having everything thought out and precisely engineered to allow for the few last second touches to dishes to be done *à la minute* instead of timing things so that ten items had to come up together; this revelation actually resulted in better food without making it harder. It was possible to run a restaurant in a calm, mindful atmosphere wherein cooks used their brains more than their bodies. Japan taught me that I could thrive in calmness. I knew that I needed to re-engineer my menus and kitchens in order to achieve this control kinesis. I remember wishing that I had seen that cooking culture at the beginning of my career; maybe then I wouldn't have ended up so tired.

Needless to say, the implementation of what I learned in Japan into my own kitchen at Cyrus wasn't done overnight. It's really hard to change culture once it's ingrained, even when you're the boss. But I was able to evolve, and I'm still practicing. There are cooks who come through my kitchens and struggle in this environment. I can see it on their faces; they appear to be disgruntled, or in distress. Their expressions communicate loud and clear to me that the work *isn't hard enough* or that they feel they aren't moving fast enough. I can sympathize. I used to feel the same way. It wasn't that long ago that I was an adrenaline junkie abusing caffeine and over-the-counter stimulants just so I could push it more. Some of the cooks who pass through just can't thrive without the volume or aggression to fuel their adrenaline. At some point, I realized that I no longer wanted to manage those types of people. I set a new standard of a healthier work environment for myself and for my team. The goals were, and still are, to create less stress, less noise, more peace, and hopefully more perfection.

And no live turtles.

CHAPTER TWENTY-SEVEN

"Superstition" (Single) by Stevie Wonder

Although slightly out of chronological order, this seems like a good place to mention that the highlight of my career to date was cooking for President Barack Obama. I had cooked for many celebrities before the Obama event, including Tom and Gisselle Brady, Justin Timberlake and Jessica Biel, Gwyneth Paltrow, Robin Williams, Sean Penn, Sharon Stone, Dennis Franz, and Bo Schembechler, to name just a few. I'd cooked for celebrities my entire career, and they never made me nervous. But with Obama, I was starstruck.

I got the call asking if I could cook for the twelve-person dinner party and, if so, what was my fee?

Really? I thought.

"You aren't paying me," I stated firmly. "I got this."

President Obama is someone I admire so deeply that I would have paid for the privilege to cook that meal. The man embodies everything that the presidency means to me. We had a great, brilliant, compassionate, thoughtful human in charge of our country for eight years. His character is something to aspire to. I was, and still am, in awe of his raw intelligence; the man operates on another level. Also, after growing up in Detroit amidst a deep, racial divide, Obama's election gave me hope that our culture was turning to a new page in our history; it made my soul happy. At the time of this dinner, I missed President

Obama in the White House terribly. If I could give him one night of nourishment and an enjoyable culinary experience for his service and inspiration, it would mean more to me than any award I could ever receive. It felt like a way for me to finally contribute something meaningful to the toxic political climate.

The meal, I was determined, would be perfect. The menu would consist of only the very best. The courses would include a variation of poke, a nod to Obama's Hawaiian roots, a playful chicken wing *lollipop,* a soba-wrapped ocean trout, and since it was white truffle season, the red wine risotto with truffles would be making an appearance. For dessert, we executed an inspired combination of Orizaba mousse, coffee ice cream, and devil's food cake hidden under a dome of uber-delicate blown-glass caramel to be shattered at the table by each guest. Our pastry chef, Mindy Beebe, had cradled the fragile sugar domes in her arms the entire eight-hour car ride from Sonoma County to Los Angeles, breathing a deep sigh after every bump we hit. We only lost two.

The preparations for the meal in the kitchen of a private home on the day of the dinner went quite smoothly, except for the moment I discovered that the mini fryer had been placed right below a small Picasso painting—yes, really, I did that. We were locked and loaded and ready to go when an Obama Foundation representative communicated that Obama would not likely be able to stay the whole time. I understood. The man had a lot of demands on his time. I'd be grateful for whatever he could afford. And, if he left early, I might dip into the epic wines being served a little sooner.

Dressed in a dark black suit with an open-collared, white dress shirt and no tie, President Obama entered the house through the back door, right into the kitchen. The energy that followed him was spectacular; the entire house changed. Even though he was smiling and appeared relaxed and casual, every muscle in my body tightened. The man was in the house. I couldn't make eye contact at first, although I'm sure he would have greeted me warmly then if I had. But I wanted to cook first.

The dinner party guests, including Jennifer Lawrence, Elon Musk,

Sean Parker, and Peter Jackson and his wife, appeared to be as starstruck as me. Valerie Jarret, Obama's longtime advisor, seemed to be the only person not in awe. It's hard to capture the atmosphere of the house. The energy was palpable, and the admiration was visible. Deep down, I think we were all hoping that Obama could save us from the disaster of Trump. I know I was. We wanted to feel hopeful again.

For the next three hours, I harnessed the greatest culinary focus of my career and pulled off a precise, perfect meal for President Barack Obama. They were having a blast in the dining room and eating all the food—*bonus!* Obama did not leave early, as I had been warned. *I hope they save some bubbles for me later*, I thought.

At the conclusion of the meal, Obama burst into the kitchen full of smiles, grabbed my hand, leaned toward me, and put his hand on my shoulder like I was his long, lost buddy.

"Chef! My man, you blew me away!"

"Thanks very much," I said, handing him a warm chocolate chip cookie.

"I'm comin' back to bring Michelle to your restaurant. It sounds incredible. Sean told me all about it."

I wanted to crack a joke that we might be too busy, or that it would be a hard table to get, but I didn't know him that well, and he hadn't actually eaten the cookie yet.

"Man, we miss you," I managed. There was so much to say, but somehow, at that moment, I couldn't find the words.

"I'm not goin' anywhere," he replied smoothly. "I'm still here."

You really are, I realized. The man's true words gave me great comfort. He was and *is* still here for the American people. He's working as hard as ever through his foundation and through meetings with people who share his passion for positive change. He never left us; he just left an address.

With a true sense of humility and service himself, Obama clearly understood how much it meant to the cooks, dishwashers, and waitstaff to have a moment of time with him. He offered to take pictures with us. I could hardly believe it. That day, the man had flown cross-country, attended a full day of meetings, had a long dinner with epic wines, and then made it a priority to give us some of his time.

"We couldn't do that," I insisted. I mean, when would I have any leverage on a president again? "We need to clean up and get back home."

Okay, I didn't really say that, but it would have been funny. Go ahead, you try to be witty around him.

Obama posed for photos until every single person had a turn. As we finished our group Cyrus photo with him and walked away, Mindy spontaneously burst into tears.

He immediately offered her a gentle hug; I think that might have happened a lot to him. It was very sweet.

"I'm sorry," Mindy said through her tears.

"It's okay," he said warmly as they separated, his hands still on her shoulders as she composed herself. "It's okay."

In that moment, he offered compassion and comfort without pretense or ego.

After the impromptu photo shoot, the entire party rolled into the kitchen. Thank God I had lots of warm, chocolate chip cookies with iced shots of milk ready. I passed those around to the billionaires, politicians, and movie stars. Pro tip, folks; just pop out some warm, chocolate chip cookies, and you'll have any guest in the world at "hello."

Those cookies transformed our relationships into something much less formal. Two feet away from me, Elon Musk was leaning against the refrigerator, cookie in hand, as he chatted with Peter Jackson's wife. They were standing next to Jennifer Lawrence, who was chatting up Barack. I managed to convince Valerie Jarrett to snap a photo with me. I had admired her for the last eight years as the president's closest advisor, and the chance to casually chat with her for a few minutes was remarkable. We just chit-chatted about wine country and promised to become Twitter buddies (FYI – I held up my end of the bargain.) The kitchen party was magical. Obama had set the tone with his casual demeanor and approachability. Everyone, the stars and the staff together, were so happy and light, just like old friends at a great party.

That night encompassed so much of what I dreamed for my career. I was great at something, and I was able to use that gift and earned skill to nourish people at an event in honor of a person I truly admire. And, I didn't have to deal with the restaurant industry problems that night. I just got to cook dinner, and it was everything I'd hoped it would be.

CHAPTER TWENTY-EIGHT

"That Lonesome Road" (Live) by James Taylor

Business was cranking at Cyrus. Plus, we had ventured into the casual segment of the restaurant business and opened up a burger joint called Healdsburg Bar and Grill, located in a prime location on the square in Healdsburg, and it was doing well. And, after two more lawsuits and settlements, David Mars and his lovely family had finally decided to sell their struggling hotel. So, we would be getting a new landlord at Cyrus.

The awards for Cyrus and for myself kept amassing. The stars were consistent, and I had been nominated for a James Beard Award for the Best Chef of California. I could feel momentum building, and I was seeing some of the fruits of the long years of labor ripen. I felt a powerful sense of duty to pay it forward. My parents had shown by example that "To whom much is given, much is expected." So, I harnessed all of the positive energy and directed every hour of time I could to charity work. I worked with Sonoma County Boys and Girls Club, San Francisco Child Abuse Center, and Healdsburg Farm to Pantry, to name a few. Basically, if someone approached me from a charity that helped feed the hungry, helped kids in need, or helped animals, I wouldn't say no. I also founded a charity with Colleen Combs, called Green Dog Rescue Project, the first predominantly non-kennel shelter facility in the United States; no more jail cell-like cages for dogs like Cash.

On the personal side, Lael and I had merged our packs, Lael with Indie, and me with my musketeers, Lola and Milo. We bought a small house on a gorgeous property overlooking the stunning views of Alexander Valley. I had managed to set up a nice life in an agricultural town that I loved and was content. I felt like if I just focused on all the positives, and there were so many, then I could overlook or at least tolerate the culinary industry issues that had me so fired up before. And I knew that I could make small differences in the industry and my restaurants by giving my staff a more positive work environment and a more humane schedule.

Then, Lola got sick, and her death spiraled me into a very dark place. The positives in my life retracted into the background. I retreated into myself. Lael understood that I needed space to grieve; she's always been able to anticipate that need in me and grant it. But one of my biggest regrets in life is that I didn't fully appreciate and indulge Milo in the months after Lola died. I didn't ignore him by any means. Lael and I loved him. But Milo was easy to take for granted. Sure, he could get right in your face, but he was also the most obedient and respectful animal on the planet. So, if you didn't engage, he would give me space. I regret asking for that space. He was a true friend and beautiful soul, and he deserved more appreciation for the wonderful creature he was. But depression had clouded my judgment, and I wasn't myself during that time. Sometimes the pain of loss felt excruciating. Other times, I just felt numb. Grief is like that, I guess.

The night I won the James Beard Award for Best Chef in California (think, a chef's version of winning Best Actor at The Oscars) should have been filled with celebration and joy, but I could barely talk. I had coveted that award as a way of cementing my legitimacy and stature as a chef. But when they announced my name that night, I trudged through the murky sea of applause and smiles from colleagues in my black-tie attire feeling only the deep depression pressing down on me like a weighted jacket. I couldn't feel anything but sadness. I would have traded that award and that night for one more day with Lola healthy.

I could barely feel anything at all anymore when the doctor told us, just months later, that Milo had heavily advanced stomach cancer. Milo was the sweetest animal I have ever met. He was a peacekeeper. We tried an intense dose of chemo via an overnight intravenous drip. The veterinarian said we should wait and hope. But the very next morning, our veterinarian called and told us that it was time to let Milo go. Milo wasn't responding, and we needed to come see him off.

The veterinary hospital had us set up in a private room. We waited for my brother and sister-in-law to show up. Milo had originally been in their household before they moved. Lying down, Milo lifted his head up and looked at each one of us in the eyes, slowly and methodically. He offered me a kiss before he lay his head back down. I was positioned behind him. The vet, sensing that I might feel left out, asked if I wanted to move around and face him.

"No," I replied. "He knows I'm here." I'd keep my hand on his back as he drifted off. We often sat like that.

After that day, I went from a bad place of numbness and depression to about as far down as I have ever sunk. I didn't want to come home anymore. I would drive down one of the most beautiful two and a half miles of road in the world with tears of grief flowing. Every morning, I had to peel off scratchy salt that had collected at the corners of my eyes overnight. Somehow, Milo's death solidified Lola's in my mind. All the hurt came together and didn't leave. The booze only helped for a short, but thankful time. Exercise didn't help. Work kind of helped as I was in extreme demand every second of the workday. But I didn't enjoy work during that time. I couldn't appreciate it, even in the peaceful environment I'd created. I couldn't appreciate anything. The industry bullshit started eating away at me again; my anger and resentment grew. At least at work, I couldn't burst into tears; there just wasn't time. Lael tried everything she could, bless her, but I was inconsolable and lost. Plus, she wasn't a dog. I used dogs in my healing process, and both of mine were gone. I know she was worried about me.

Stan was worried, too. He took me to In and Out Burger a lot.

He wasn't afraid to approach the delicate subject, but then he'd try to get me to laugh.

So, he'd drag my woes out of me, and then say, "Okay, enough about you," or "Oh my God, stop talking."

Other times, he'd call me under the pretense of needing to ask a question about something and then hang up when I was mid-sentence in response.

Then, I'd call back and say, "Stan, I have a question," and *click,* immediately hang up on him. It was a game we'd play.

Other times, he'd call and ask if I wanted to bet on a game. "Okay," he'd say. "Two dollars. I'll tell you who I pick after." *Click.*

Within a week, I'd get two dollars in quarters in the mail.

If you are as lucky as I am, you will find a mentor who will be there when your entire family falls apart in divorce. Or, if you are as lucky as I am, your mentor will be someone who will drive from Washington, DC during the brutal winters to Michigan every other week to check on you, as you provide the primary care for your dying father and his best friend. Or, if you are lucky, like me, it will be someone who will jump into action and locate and befriend the world's best brain surgeon when you are diagnosed with a brain tumor right smack dab in your motor pathway. Or, possibly, you will find a mentor who will drive two hours to sit with you as you and your wife put your dog, Lola, down, hug you, and drive away as silently as he arrived, never expecting a thing in return.

I knew I was lucky to have Stan at my side, and he did make me laugh; but not even Stan could help rid me of my depression during that time. Depression is like a blanket you can't get off. There's no out and no positive thought. Depression adds momentum to itself; it spirals. Losing my canine companions was more than the grief I'd experienced when I lost my dad. This was different altogether. I could not get out of myself and release the grip of depression.

CHAPTER TWENTY-NINE

"Somewhere Over The Rainbow" by Israel Kamakawiwo'ole

Sometimes the people who love you know you best, even if you don't want them to. Around six months after Milo left us, Lael started to pester me about a dog she had found somewhere in the Bay Area.

"No fucking way. I can't."

The mere thought of replacing Lola and Milo made me slip into a crying jag that would start yet another tailspin of dark thoughts and inconsolable moods. I don't know how many times she put this dog's picture in my face, but I couldn't bring myself to feel for him or even look at him for any length of time.

"No. I don't want another lab." Maxie and Lola were labs.

"But he's so young, and he's been abandoned, and he needs help," she pleaded.

I held firm. "No. I don't want a puppy. Puppies always get adopted, and they're a shit ton of work."

"Can we just go meet him, Doug? I really want to."

I don't know if Milo, Maxie, and Lola's spirits got together that evening in my dreams and told me it was okay to go meet the little blond bomber known as Rico, or if I had a change of heart because I learned that Rico would soon need rehab from a scheduled knee surgery in the near future. But either way, I caved, and off we went to Dublin, California, a painful three-hour drive from Alexander Valley.

As we settled into the room to wait to meet him, Alastair the veterinarian spent a few minutes going over his history. The people who had Rico originally had dropped him off to be euthanized at five months due to his bad knee that needed immediate surgery. Alastair had already known Rico via some elbow work. He asked the people to surrender Rico to him as he was willing to do the surgery and find him a home. Alastair let it be known that he wasn't that fond of labs in general, but that this one was special.

Rico bounded into the room with a burst of bull-like energy paired with the cutest face ever, with a permanent crease on the ridge of his nose. Someone forgot to tell him he couldn't walk well; that bad knee just needed to try and keep up with him. Rico wasn't stopping for any pain, and he had a mosh pit with a chef from Healdsburg to jump into. He was intense, funny, confident, sweet, and had a spirit that resonated with me from the first drunken sailor hop into the room. He claimed me instantly.

I looked at Lael with tears in my eyes and said, "Okay."

I don't know if she was surprised by how quickly it happened or if she knew all along that once I agreed to meet him, the deal would be done.

We spent about fifteen minutes just playing in the office. I knew there was another side to this never-ending gobstopper of energy in the form of a technically lame lab that we hadn't yet seen. I was waiting for the hurricane of love to end and watch his mellow kick in. It had to be exhausting to be stuck in a kennel, nursing a hurt knee, and not knowing what happened to Mom and Dad. Then, just like that, he collapsed with his full weight into the contours of my waiting love. I wasn't the softest or flattest dog bed, but I was his. My heart was open again, and it felt like I suddenly had a lot of room in there. I felt Milo and Lola jump off my shoulder and head off to a green field with a lake where Maxie was. At that moment, I knew that I would be okay.

We didn't get to take Rico home that day as he desperately needed the surgery. We bid farewell, which was pretty hard to do even though we had just met, to our new family member with a date to pick him up in six days. And don't worry, I changed his name to Finnegan Keane (from Dublin, of course).

From that day forward, Finnegan Keane had a new best friend in me. If we weren't recovering from one of Finn's many surgeries (he was given a bad body from the start, and we knew what we had signed up for), we were laughing together. A simple walk to the mailbox was an adventure in acorn harvesting. A swim in the pool prompted wrestling afterwards.

He went to work with me; he drove with me. He was the best friend I could ever ask for. He did not accept that there could be sadness in this world, and yet he insisted that I be with him when I was sad. We would lock eyes whenever we had been apart for a short while, signaling that everything was okay at that moment. He could illicit a smile out of me instantaneously, no matter the time of day or the situation.

Finn could also speak. *"Woo, woo, woo"* in three different octaves meant *hello* to the person who just showed up, obviously to visit Finny. One low *"Woo—grrr"* meant *it's time to wake up and eat.* If the *grrr* was replaced by a grunt, it meant he had to pee, but also, *could we eat after?*

Finnegan was also my bait dog for training the tougher cases at Green Dog. The dogs that couldn't socialize with other dogs were my favorite cases. I knew it wasn't their fault; some human had fucked them up. So, I was determined to bring out their best no matter how long it took. What took me months of work would take Finnegan fifteen seconds to accomplish when I got out of his way. He would walk into a pen with an aggressive dog and immediately become friends. You could see the joy on the other dogs' faces and body language. They would initially nip or snap, or do even worse sometimes, but Finny would never respond negatively. There was playing to do and food to eat and hugs to get, after all. *Come on dude, relax. No need to growl. Let's go play!*

My favorite time with Finny was the one-on-one time we had after his surgeries. The trust he put in me to let me help was soul-satisfying. His friendship was a gift I could never quantify. I only wish he knew how often he saved me and healed my pains. The late night mosh pits on the carpet in the walk-in closet (converted from a bedroom when Lael and I decided that we would not have kids, and we didn't really like long-term guests) were what my vision of heaven was and still is. I would give anything for one more furry love fest on that floor. The two knee surgeries, two elbow excavations, and multiple spinal surgeries never dampened our spirits. We were both happy to spend the time together when we were at our best and our worst.

To be clear, Finnegan Keane wasn't *my* dog at all; he was my buddy and my best friend. He made everyone laugh who met him, and he kept me from crashing back down into deep depression many times. And he helped me to regain myself in a way no person ever could. I am forever grateful to have had the privilege of experiencing a friendship with such a positive soul.

With Finnegan Keane's inspiration, I searched for a positive, new goal on which to refocus my mental energy. The entire Cyrus team, with my direction, decided to open a Japanese-inspired steakhouse, Shimo, right next door to Healdsburg Bar and Grill, and just down the street from Cyrus. Healdsburg didn't have a steakhouse yet, which was unusual because a steakhouse is a staple for most towns. My thought was that all we had to do was throw in the abundance of red wine from the nearby wineries; it was almost a no-brainer. *Shimo* means *frost* in Japanese, and in terms of steak, it refers to the look of the white marbling of fat throughout a steak and the grading of the steak in quality. Had we opened a traditional steak house with traditional side dishes and sauces, we probably would have been fine. But I don't like doing things that have already been done. It's part of my DNA to push the envelope and be creative. Life's more fun and rewarding when you're making your own rules. The downside is that when it crashes, and your name is in the big lights, the whole world gets to peer deep inside you and tell you that you're an idiot. At least, it feels like that.

Instead of opening a traditional steakhouse, I created a Japanese-influenced steakhouse with flavors and ingredients that spoke to me. I desperately wanted to change the traditional approach to steakhouses in America with their massive, oversized portions of average beef with massive, oversized portions of heavy starches on the side. Fat on fat, heavy on heavy, and finish it off with cheesecake. I had learned in Japan that I could satiate people with umami and keep them interested with acid. I realized that I felt better after a big meal that enlisted fewer carbs and less fat. The use of umami made up for the lack of carbs, and the use of ultra-high-quality beef (protein) meant that a person could eat much less and still feel nourished and satisfied. (Think Mr. Miyagi doing wax on, wax off, versus Homer Simpson with a belly rub.) With the help of a brilliant chef I hired, Kolin Vazzoler, we created dishes that utilized those principles and buffed out the meats with gorgeous vegetables, sides, and sauces that took advantage of acid instead of all the traditional American butter-laden sauces.

The naked part is that a lot of thought, soul, and effort went into creating Shimo. It wasn't an ego play. It was an attempt to do something different and give my vision of a steakhouse to the area. It was an invitation to my local community to join me on a new culinary ride that I believed they would like. I wanted them to experience a three-ounce, A-5 Wagyu with yuzu-kosha butter and an okonomiyaki (savory Japanese pancake). The whole team at Shimo bought into the vision, and we were excited to offer our fare.

The funny thing is, sometimes when someone has some success, there are other people out there hoping to see failure. Over time, I got pretty good at brushing off the negativity aimed at me by using it for inspiration to work harder and to do better for others. *Hold my beer, pal. I got this.* But this time, the cuts hurt. About a week or two before we opened Shimo, I found Lael, who was managing the restaurant, in tears in the Shimo office holding a handwritten note that had been attached to the front door by some local urchin. The letter began by stating that this unnamed and spineless person was a local, and that (s)he wanted us to know that (s)he was rooting for our failure and counting the days until we closed. We hadn't even opened yet, and this idiot wanted us closed. (S)he couldn't even say my food sucked. The fact that we were trying something different and coloring outside the lines really irked him or her so much that they felt the need to write an anonymous, nasty note. This coward caused Lael, who doesn't have bad thoughts about *anyone*, to break into tears and wonder how someone could hate her so much. We had raised the money, we hired locals, we paid local contractors to help us redecorate, we were giving local farms business, and, oh, we LIVED HERE, TOO. Between our three restaurants, we employed close to a hundred people. We were trying to do good for and within our community. Apparently, that anonymous local didn't get that.

Unfortunately, the first naysayer wasn't the only one. A few months after we opened, one of our business neighbors, Charles, who owned a sausage restaurant called The Wurst (get it?), decided to tell me how happy he was that my place would soon be closing.

This little human stood toe-to-toe with me and screamed, "I can't wait to see what the next business will be that takes over after you have to let all of your employees go and close up!"

I stood there, incredulous. *You are in the same business as me, and you know how tough it is. When you opened, I sent people to you, and I even ate your shitty, mass-produced, non-local, overcooked sausages because I wanted you to make it. And now, you want me to close and lose money, and you want my employees to lose their jobs?*

It's that type of cruelty that still eats at me these many years later. I'd love a few seconds with the local who wanted us to close before we opened. I'd like Lael to get a chance to ask him how many jobs he's created in his life? How many risks has he taken? What's his passion?

Failure is a part of everyone's life and business. Restaurants are notorious for high failure rates. I learned my freshman year at Cornell that nine in ten restaurants close in the first year. And those that make it past that first year don't fare much better. Most are gone after five years. And the standard profit margins in the restaurant business don't make it a safe harbor for hard-earned cash. It's great luck to bring 20 percent to the bottom line at a restaurant. Ten percent is considered healthy for most restaurants. The higher end and smaller restaurants usually coincide with a dwindling profit margin. Cook burgers for seven hundred or so people a day, and you might get up to 25 percent profit. But if you choose to make foie gras and truffles for eighty-five people, then 10 to 20 percent is fantastic.

Some restaurants just close because it's time. Maybe they had a good run, but the lease was about to expire, and another five years wasn't looking like a lot of fun. For others, the food and service just sucked, and people stopped coming. Some run out of money due to a slow beginning and just can't hold on any longer. Some have good food and good service, but for some reason, can't seem to catch fire. It's a tricky business, and there isn't a formula—except for the chains, which pretty much know how they are going to perform. Restaurant chains are in the business of restaurants—not the restaurant business. The restaurant business encompasses the rest of us independent thinkers and gamblers willing to try something different, something with passion. Open a Red Lobster or a Rutherford Grill and you will get higher profit margins and good returns. But you won't get much soul. I'm not saying that all chain food is bad or not edible by any means. They serve a purpose and a segment of the market that truly couldn't care less about exploring the world of cuisine. I get it, and I don't begrudge it one bit. I eat at restaurants like these (In and Out Burger has my loyalty), and I eat mac n' cheese out of a box at home (it's delicious). But in the spirit of one of my all-time favorite movies, *Things to Do in Denver When you are Dead*, I would rather buckwheat myself than live in a soulless, passionless world.

With all that failure built into the dysfunctional business model of restaurants, you would think that it's expected when a restaurant doesn't make it. Well, in the greater scheme of things, it is. But when it's yours, it really hurts. It's the kind of hurt that causes you to question your intelligence, your skill level, your integrity, and whether or not you should do the work anymore. The guilt of having to tell people that they aren't going to have a job soon can take you to a very dark, lonely place. The ego takes a hit, and the press release brings no joy. It's hard to say "I suck" with much spin.

Shimo was an epic failure, but not necessarily in terms of money, as our investors were fully reimbursed (except myself and my two partners). Our concept and execution just didn't connect with foodies, and for the life of me I still can't figure it out. It wasn't a bad location; my Healdsburg Bar and Grill was thriving right next door. It wasn't the food. We had great ingredients, a great crew, and great service. The concept just didn't work. Not enough people understood what we were trying to do.

When I finally saw the light, there was a peaceful shame that took over. *I suck. I can't figure it out. I have to close. There isn't any more money to keep it going, and there's nothing else to try anyway. It's just not going to work.* That decision was kind of easy in a weird way just like having brain surgery was an easy decision because I didn't really have a choice. But telling the staff was incredibly hard. The failure was on me. I tried to help them out as much as possible. We offered everyone a job at our other restaurants.

I think the hardest part is knowing that there are plenty of people out there like the anonymous local and the sausage douche. Are they jealous, angry, or just eternally miserable with themselves? I guess it's not for me to figure out; I just need to process it and move on.

It takes a little while to recover from that type of business heartbreak. I didn't want to push the boundaries at all for a while. I wanted to lick my wounds. People try to say that the restaurant business is art. I've always called bullshit back on that notion. Yes, there is an artistic side, for sure. But with real art, the artist keeps on painting or sculpting whether or not they sell anything. A restaurant doesn't have that option. If people don't want to buy your steak, you close. Sometimes, I think it might be nice to just go home and not put myself out there anymore. It sure seems like a better option than opening a Red Lobster. Closing Shimo definitely yanked me down from my work utopia. Sometimes all the stupid comes for you at once.

CHAPTER THIRTY

"The Rocky Road to Dublin" by The Dubliners

After five years of dealing with David Mars and his family as the owners of Les Mars, it was welcome news to me via my friend Chris Williams that a billionaire by the name of Bill Foley wanted to buy the hotel with us. *Finally!* It was a real possibility to make the hotel and restaurant one cohesive unit. I hadn't heard the name Bill Foley before, but Chris assured me that he was a good guy. If this Foley had cash, wanted a small hotel, and understood the level Cyrus was operating on, then I would be in.

I did a little research on Bill before our first meeting at Shimo just before its opening; we had some privacy. It was obvious that he knew how to make money. He had started Fidelity National Financial, a big financial real estate services company, and he had plenty of other interests. Recently, he had made a move into the wine business (Sonoma and other areas), thus igniting his interest in a small hotel in Healdsburg.

All I wanted was for the guy to put up the money to buy the hotel *with us* and let us run it. We were full-on in our heyday of Cyrus. The idea of making a truly world class experience at Les Mars with Cyrus overseeing it seemed organic and exciting. It was such a small hotel, with just sixteen rooms, that the only way to make it work from a financial and operational perspective was to combine efficiencies with the restaurant and operate it as one entity. We knew it. Also, at that point, Cyrus was, by far, the best luxury brand in Sonoma County. Anyone who had common sense and any desire to buy the hotel would come and talk to us first.

At the meeting, Bill then casually dropped the tidbit that he had "already bought the hotel . . . kind of."

What the FUCK? The awkwardness in the room was seasoned with my worst poker face. I couldn't understand why he do this without checking with me. *I* had brought the deal to *him*. It would have taken just a simple email to Chris or me. He explained that it was a business move to "take it off the market" and that the only risk was a small deposit he had to put up. We chatted for about thirty minutes or so and the vibe never really clicked. It just seemed that we had different goals, and it would be hard to align them in my opinion. We ended the meeting quickly but cordially. Bill and Chris were coming into Cyrus that night to have dinner, but I sincerely hoped and expected that once Bill figured out that it wasn't the right chemistry with us that he might get his deposit back and we could move on to hopefully find a more suitable partner.

There were a few phone calls later among the elders (Nick and Bill), to see if we had any common ground but it was obvious that no deal could be made.

Bill went quiet for a while, and we assumed he lost interest and moved on. And then, he resurfaced in an email from his new partner, David Fink, a restaurateur and hotelier based out of Carmel, California, someone Nick and I were familiar with. Fink let us know that they had bought the hotel. Fink said that he and Foley needed to sit down with us because they wanted us to provide some services for their sixteen-room hotel.

Now, I'm going to give you a quick hotel restaurant lesson here for free. A high-end hotel needs food and beverage services, and they need them seven days a week and sometimes twenty-four hours a day. A two-star Michelin restaurant that is open for five days a week for dinner doesn't jibe with that schedule. A sixteen-room hotel requires sixteen breakfasts at best, and how much room service do you think it requires? Very minimal. So, Cyrus could not expand the staff to fulfill round-the-clock service needs when the resulting income stream would be so miniscule. We'd lose a ton of money. We had explained this to both Mars and Foley. *No fucking way. Zero desire.*

If, on the other hand, we were part owners of the hotel operations and part of the real estate and the entire business, then we would have gladly taken on those types of services, and we would have done them efficiently and with excellence by combining staffs. But remember when Bill bought the hotel without us? Yeah, I did too.

"Sorry, David (Fink)," I replied, "We aren't interested in talking. Best of luck to you and Bill."

The next few years were pretty typical from my perspective, unfortunately. There was no way to agree. If you're really curious, you can look it up using the following key words: CYRUS, BILL FOLEY, DAVID FINK, EVICTION, LAWSUIT. Yep. There are depositions, emails, testimony, and press articles. The press took a keen interest in it due to all the players involved.

I wanted nothing more than to stop this fiasco and just focus on Cyrus and our other projects. And let Fink and Foley run their hotel. The *San Francisco Chronicle* articles generated a huge amount of publicity. Of course, the newspaper asked Fink for a statement in response. Fink then commented that they were looking forward to working with us, and that the eviction notice was a misunderstanding. *Great*, I thought. *We can move on and coexist.*

Things never settled down between us and eventually Bill and I met at his winery, Chalk Hill, to see if we could settle our differences before one of us filed a lawsuit. I went to the meeting to mainly listen and to deliver a very clear message.

When it was my turn to talk, I stated simply, "I think you realize now that this hotel doesn't work without the restaurant, but the restaurant works without the hotel. If you want to buy Cyrus, then let's talk. We can discuss a price and then talk about whether or not we stay on."

"Yeah, let's do that," he replied.

I think Bill was sincere in wanting to set aside our differences and figure something out. From my perspective these types of disagreements are exhausting. I can only assume he felt the same way and would like to focus on positive things. At least it seemed so from our peace summit.

I also needed to let him know that Cyrus was our everything. And that we would defend ourselves in every possible way.

"Bill, you know how everyone talks about how nasty and tough al-Qaeda is in their fighting?"

He laughed as I paused, thinking that was the end of my point.

"Well," I continued, "al-Qaeda is a bunch of pussies compared to the IRA (Irish Republican Army). Think of me as the IRA if we go to battle."

I believe Bill caught my sincerity. Foley is an Irish name, after all.

We discussed communicating again soon about a potential deal to see if we could resolve the differences amicably and put to rest all the legal tactics and expenses.

I stood, offered my hand; he accepted, and I said goodbye as I walked out.

We didn't come to a deal, unfortunately.

Eighteen months and a lengthy lawsuit later, Nick and I walked out of a mediation with Foley, having negotiated, (in totality) approximately a four-million-dollar deal to part ways. We also kept the name Cyrus, our dignity, and our freedom. We made more money on that settlement than we could have made if we had stayed for the next ten-plus years we had left on that lease. And I made sure that we got to stay through our busiest season before we closed our doors so that we could still collect that cash and distribute it to our investors and our staff.

There is so much more that could be said about those times, but this line from the settlement agreement does it best:

"The Parties will not disparage or make derogatory statements about each other or the business practices of each other orally or in writing."

Enough said.

So, I guess we won? We got a lot of money; the investors got a lot of money; and the employees all got taken care of. But I lost the dream. And all the drama of those ten years had taken its toll on me. I was worn down. It's exhausting to run a business that needs to perform on the highest of levels and simultaneously fight off lawsuits. I had great support from Nick, Drew, and our lawyer and partner, Barbara Gordon. With the addition of my brother, Chris, jumping into the sandbox, he and Barbara were able to fend off the multiple legal armadas over the years.

The motivation I had accumulated from all of my positive experiences cooking for inspiring people and learning from mentors who taught me to pay it forward had withered. Instead of focusing on how I could grow and contribute, I was just trying to make it through each day and manage my anger. When the fight was over, I had to come to terms with losing Cyrus, and losing Lola and Milo. I could feel the depression grabbing tighter each day. And I didn't like myself.

CHAPTER THIRTY-ONE

"Lonely is the Night"
by Billy Squier

I'd had enough bourbon that I'm surprised I could even find my truck in the parking garage. There was a free hotel room waiting for me ten yards away. It would have been so easy: check in, take aspirin, drink water, pass out, wake up, and drive home the next morning. That's how it should have played out. I do NOT drink and drive. But I did that night. And it wasn't a matter of possibly having one too many. I was ten or twelve past my limit.

I slipped the oversized plastic key into the ignition of my 1997, burgundy F-150 with two hundred thousand miles on it. I popped some Dentyne Ice gum out of its foiled chambers to alleviate dry mouth from the bourbon. I fumbled my late-night driving glasses on and squinted to unblur my vison. I pulled out onto Pacific Avenue with liquored-fueled arrogance and headed towards the Golden Gate Bridge with seventy-plus miles to go. As my playlist shuffled between Irish rebel drinking songs and the *Les Misérables* soundtrack, tears welled, blurring my vision again. When Jean Valjean asked, "Who am I?" over the stereo, I was jealous that he had an answer. He was 24601. I, on the other hand, had just been hit with the searing reality that I wasn't at all the person I thought I was.

I wouldn't have been able to forgive myself if I had hurt someone that night. But I wouldn't have minded if I had gotten hurt. Feeling something real and intense would have been a welcome sharp cut compared to the overwhelming sense of numb, paralyzing confusion that had been bubbling in me over time and had finally boiled over that night.

It was a clear, late July night, and crisp in the way San Francisco can be in the summer. I cracked the window just a bit to allow a sobering breeze in to help keep me focused. My body was somehow driving that truck. My tired and non-obedient right foot kept slipping off the gas pedal, impaired from booze and residually injured from brain surgery, and these slips caused sudden jerk reactions that kept me awake. My chest was tight. It was hard to catch a breath—the beginning of a heavy, slow-approaching, asthmatic episode. *Just focus on the outbreath. The inbreath will take care of itself*, I coached myself.

I had just escaped from the first ever Four-Star Dinner event organized by the *San Francisco Chronicle*. All nine of the Bay Area's four-star anointed chefs were cordially invited to prepare a course, under the cover of charity, in Michael Bauer's honor for his 25th Anniversary as the *Chronicle's* longtime restaurant critic. This dinner, in some skewed, self-justified, self-entitled light, seemed like an appropriate ending to an illustrious eight-year run at my very own four-star restaurant, Cyrus. For as long as I can remember, my only goal, personal and professional, was to achieve four stars. My time had been charted by watching the awarding of stars. Who got four? Who lost one? Who deserved more? Four stars meant the best of the best.

When I attained four stars at Cyrus, I achieved my dream. Then, after seven years with those stars, I found myself in the middle of shutting it down after the lengthy and exhausting legal battle. That's when I was asked to cook in Bauer's honor with all of the elites in one kitchen. There would be nine top chefs who were all used to running a kitchen their way, trying to work in the same kitchen at the same time. What could go wrong?

If I had a shred of dignity left at that point, I would have said no way to the dinner. In fact, I probably had the most power to decline out of all of the chefs. I would be, in effect, giving my stars back by closing Cyrus. I really could have said no. The other chefs were still in the game, and no way in hell could they offend the Grand Poohbah by declining.

But when I was asked, I summoned up all my Midwest ethics and replied, "Sounds great. I'd be honored." Yeah, I added the *honored* part all on my own; what a pansy. My long-suppressed dignity whispered from the rafters, *It's for charity*.

I had plenty of thoughts about how fucked up this dinner was on its face. First off, the attention-shy Michael Bauer was not leaving the game. On Monday evening he would be right back to bestowing everyone's stars under some anonymous cover. *Would a chef lose a star for not participating? Probably not.* But it was an unwritten rule, what I now realize is part of the sick restaurant culture, that every one of us would take this pressure as part of our job. Would it be noticed if one of us said no to the dinner? Hell yeah. And who had the guts to risk what that could possibly mean? Not any of us. Not me. Even if I was leaving the game. Bauer could make you or break you.

Despite my ambivalence, I had also longed for this dinner, worked hard for it my entire adult life, and deserved it. In fact, I was excited about it. I was a four-star chef at the top of my game and being recognized for that. So yeah, I knew the dinner had a rancid odor, but I wanted the smell. This contradiction caused its own painful reality. There's a type of guilty awareness when you actually realize you are part of a cult but not sure if you can really leave.

I showed up on time. I always show up on time; Midwest upbringing. The dinner was at Quince, a newly minted four-star, obviously leveraged to offer up their space for the event as the newest member of the group. *Pay your dues, bro.* As I thought about how cool it was that all of us chefs could watch each other cook and enjoy the four-star title even if we were in bondage to Bauer, it never occurred to me that this event would drastically alter my perception of the industry, myself, and my compadres. I didn't realize how fragile I was at the time.

Before I dive into this sordid tale, please note that I decided to obscure the identities of my counterparts who participated in the event I did it because this chapter isn't about them; it's about me. They were just doing their jobs the best they could. And until very recently, I was very much the same as they were. I respected them then, and I still do. The game changed a lot of us. And just because I was having a moment of reckoning and awareness doesn't mean that they should be called out, too. No, this night was about where I went wrong, and that's no one else's fault but mine.

Before the hors d'oeuvres started, the self-appointed elder statesmen of our four-star clique, let's call him FS1 for four-star one, walked into the room and decided to hold a lineup. It wasn't his restaurant, we didn't work for him, and we all had the same four stars. But FS1, in his white, V-neck T-shirt, apparently felt that we needed some motivation. Or he just wanted to hear himself talk, receiving lots of stars will do that to you.

After the Tony Robbins of chefs excused us, things got really weird. FS2 was hitting up FS3 about how to register higher on the San Pellegrino 50 Best List, a revered ranking voted on by chefs and industry writers. FS2 pleaded with FS3 to give him the secret to how he scored so high. Since FS4 seemed to be cooking his filets of beef at room temperature for ninety-four hours, he joined the discussion. As wafts of roasting beef and body odor offended my olfactory senses, the phrase, "How do we move up the list?" was parroted among those men over and over like a bad song on repeat.

Next, FS1 grabbed FS3 and pulled him in close. I think FS1 was going for a dramatic Marlon Brando effect.

"I want to talk to you about Michelin," FS1 said in a Brando-worthy tone.

They snuck away for fifteen minutes or so. FS3 returned a little starry-eyed. He volunteered that Michelin wanted to talk to him in Paris per FS1. I don't even know if that was true or even possible.

Why couldn't they just enjoy one night, *my last* night under the big tent? Why couldn't we *all* be satisfied with what we had? I sank into myself. If there had been a dog at the event, I would have laid down on the floor and medicated with furry hugs and kisses. But no such luck. So, I put out my course by myself with no help; so much for camaraderie and four-star bonding. After my dish of Black River caviar, cauliflower panna cotta, sea urchin and dashi gelée, the powers that be marched me out like a circus animal so that I could kiss Bauer's ring in the dining room. We exchanged awkward pleasantries. What was he supposed to say? I knew I'd nailed it.

I then crawled out of my body and watch the dysfunctional marathon meal from a safe distance. None of the chefs needed help anyway; they had all brought plenty of hands. I grabbed a big drink, saddled up next to Paolo Luchessi, who was documenting the event for the *Chronicle*, and watched the dinner unfold.

Right around the time FS4 was slow basting his still unfinished beef tenderloin—it was stunning and didn't bleed a drop when sliced—I figured out why I was nauseous and so disgusted with my fellow four-star friends. We were all the same. We all shared the same pathetic need to be told we were great at something. These chefs, who I deeply respected for their work ethics, skill levels, and passions, were all just like me—needy, accolade-jonesing bagatelles. We were at the top of our games, and we couldn't be happy because we always needed more recognition, more praise, more validation.

As these thoughts of self-awareness and disgust simultaneously filled my head, I grabbed another bourbon. At that moment, I knew that I was both the symptom and the disease.

Despite or because of all that bourbon, it had occurred to me that the dinner wasn't the true problem. Straw that broke the back? Yeah, it was a clarifying moment; earnest people were doing their best within the twisted circumstances they found themselves in, which was to pay homage to their kingmaker. That word *circumstances* is the key. Something as dubiously ethical as this dinner was treated as blasé, just another part of a tough job. I felt uglier in this awareness. There were not any pups to comfort, but there was an open bar. So I drank. The step-by-step awareness of my participation and collaboration sent me over the top and into the midnight air filled with self-loathing. Why couldn't I let it go? Because I had internalized the values of a broken industry.

As the dinner played out over the next few hours the thoughts and an accompanying sharp pain came one by one.

I had always wanted four stars. I'd do anything to get them. I made lots of sacrifices, did plenty of politicking, kept my mouth shut. *Another drink.*

There was the time I debated if I could take time off work to go take care of my dying father. *Drink.*

There was the time I had to explain to a long-term sous chef that his little brother's graduation wasn't worth missing a busy weekend of work for. *Drink.*

There were all the brutal battles with landlords that I won by leveraging all my power, which brought out even more of my ugliness. *Drink.*

What happened to the nice kid from the Midwest? *Drink.*

The countless times I justified paying cooks and dishwashers as little as possible because it was the norm. I mean I worked for shit pay, why shouldn't they? *Drink.*

The *Chronicle* had secured every chef his own hotel room that night; some hotel apparently needed to kiss the *Chronicle's* ass, too. I had planned on sleeping in the city and partying one last time with the chefs and the chef-seekers who paid for the dinner and the privilege to buy us beers at the after party. Lael wasn't expecting me home. She was most likely curled up with a couple of puppies who had taken my place for the night in our bed. But I couldn't stand being in that restaurant for another minute. I couldn't stand myself. I grabbed one more quick bourbon and made an Irish exit.

When my truck pulled off Highway 101 at the Lytton Station exit, it finally registered how stupid I had been to get behind the wheel. The panic hit, and a cold sweat tacked my shirt to my numb skin. I pulled over to the area near the exit usually reserved for the taco lunch truck.

I caught my breath and turned off the music as cold San Francisco air mingled with the ninety-five-degree Sonoma summer night. Was the panic attributed to the alcohol poisoning or to the sobering reality of what had I become? I just needed to get home to Lael and Finnegan. With only a few short miles to go, I sent out a tearful plea to my guardian angel dad to get me home safely.

I awkwardly stabbed the gas pedal, the gravel sprayed, and a shot of adrenalin coursed through me. I drove the short remainder in silence, windows open. The hangover approached fast as I drove up our steep, dirt driveway and tried to figure out what I'd tell Lael.

"Are you okay?" she asked when my noisy arrival woke her. Her tone was less judgmental than I expected, and much less than I wanted. "Wow, you smell like bourbon. Did you drive?"

"Yep. Sorry. I had to come home."

She let me be. I could tell she knew I wasn't right, but she was tired, and I'm not easy to take care of, for a human.

I sat on the floor with Finnegan, my always happy, perpetually injured, white Labrador rescue and best friend. He licked the tears from my face. He didn't mind my boozy smell. I passed out on the floor with him. No dreams that night.

What I had expected to be a crowning professional achievement instead had become a moment of personal reconciliation. I had wanted a four-star restaurant my whole life. I did it; I got one, but the mask was wearing thin.

CHAPTER THIRTY-TWO

"She Talks to Angels" by The Black Crowes

When I woke up the morning after the Four-Star Bauer Dinner, I remembered coming home, lying on the floor with Finny, and crying myself to sleep as he tended to me. My head hurt pretty bad, but not like after brain surgery; that was a focused pain. This pain throbbed, but it also had metastasized to my heart and soul. I couldn't, for the life of me, figure out how I had gone from being on top of the world in my career to wanting to hurt myself.

Was it the insane hours built up over more than two decades? My exhaustion was physical and mental. Was it the marathon of lawsuits? I knew they had taken a toll. Was it that I had not kept my post-brain surgery promise to myself about living a healthier life? I knew that my physical health was deteriorating at a frightening rate, and that morning, I finally realized that my mental health was, too. How much did the broken industry play a part in all of this? I originally joined the industry because I found joy in feeding people, but then my work in the industry got twisted and somehow became focused on ego and self-adulation instead. Or was it everything brewing together for so long that the elements altogether eventually became the perfect storm?

I was grateful to be on the floor with my best friend, Finnegan Keane, instead of lying in a morgue or in a police station. I was grateful that Lael had anticipated my need for a new best friend and had found

Finnegan before that awful night. (Lael knows me better than I know myself.) Finnegan did not accept that there could be sadness, and yet he insisted that he be with me when I was sad. Over time, Finnegan would help pull me from my depression by reminding me that life is good.

I was also grateful that morning for Lael being a loving, supportive wife. Lael brought me coffee, gave me a hug and said, "I'm glad you're alright. Please don't do that again. We want you around."

My mind raced through memories of family, friends, and mentors who had helped me on my way to making my dream a reality with Cyrus. I decided right then and there on the floor with Finny, my coffee, and Cash, who had then joined us, that from that low point in my life, I was going to take the first step back to creating positive change. It was the first time in a very long time that I was able to be grateful for all of the good in my life; the phrase returned to me like a long-lost friend: *To whom much is given, much is expected.* That was the positive thing I could believe in. I had a *duty* to use all that I'd been given over the years to help others.

I had helped numerous charities and opened Green Dog Rescue Project, but I knew full well that I could do more. There are more animals and people to help every day. That would be my path to a healthier place, a healthier life, and a truly happy life. I knew it that morning. I really didn't have a clue where to begin, but I knew that I was beginning. And I knew that I could leverage the closing of Cyrus over the next few months to help forge a new path for whatever version 2.0 of myself and Cyrus would be.

It had been agreed upon at the settlement that we would keep the closing a secret until a mutually agreed upon press release date. The night before making the announcement, I called Drew and asked him to meet me in the bar at Cyrus. We were closed that day, so the entire space would be ours to chat. I felt somewhat guilty that I hadn't told Drew yet. The settlement was over two months old, and Drew, as the most invested member of our team, should have known. Drew's wife, Cynthia, was a captain at Cyrus and friends with the other servers.

Telling Drew about the closing presented too great a risk that the news would leak prematurely. So, I kept the secret until that evening.

Drew was an indispensable cog in this four-star wheel. He was also a friend, and we had worked together for over ten years. There was a chance, because the future wasn't clear, that our time working together might be over. Deep down, I didn't think it would be the last time we worked together. But you never know, and I wasn't sure where my career was headed. I wasn't sure I would even cook again. I was that undecided at that moment. I hadn't yet remembered that cooking was (and still is now as I write) my vocation.

Drew showed up at the bar right on time, and I gave him a big hug. I knew he loved bourbon, so I told him to go behind the bar and grab whatever he wanted so we could have a drink together. I never drank from the bar and never took anything without paying for it out of respect for our investors. Nick and I always thought we needed to set that example for our staff. I don't know if we ever even discussed our philosophy about that, but we both lived by it. So, when I told Drew to grab whatever he wanted to drink and pour us a stiff one, he knew something was up.

Of course he picked the Pappy Van Winkle, our most expensive and exclusive bourbon. I think he grabbed a few different bottles, a tasting, I guess. *Why not?* As we slid into the red, upholstered bar chairs, I glanced down at the sparkling travertine marble floor and the golden, Venetian plaster walls and laughed to myself about how I never really liked the way Cyrus looked. It was a little stuffy and dated for my modern design preferences. I wasn't going to miss the faux French building it was housed in, either.

We clinked our glasses together, shared an eye lock of two good friends, then sipped the brown liquid that had been just teased with a chill of the perfect ice cubes we served at Cyrus. I was surprised by how smooth it was—pleasant, caramel, warm in my throat, but not hot. I took a mindful second and savored it.

Most people dread delivering bad news, dragging it on way too long because of their discomfort. But it's more painful to the recipient that way. My advice is to just deliver the bad news as quickly as possible. Grow a sack, put the elephant on the table, and say it as nicely as you can. That way, you'll put everyone out of their misery as soon as possible. If the recipient of the bad news is surprised, then either that person is an idiot, or you didn't do your job right. It's that simple. In my situation with Drew that night, Drew wasn't technically getting fired, but the same rules applied. Besides, I knew that if I didn't get it out fast, then the Pappy would have gotten the best of me sooner or later. That would have opened the door to the possibility of Drew and I walking over to the Les Mars lobby and pissing on the potted plants lining the entrance.

I looked at Drew with tears building and said, "Unfortunately, brother, it's the end of this magnificent Cyrus ride."

Boom. Just like that. More than twelve years of dreaming and star chasing was about to end. Wonder Twin powers, deactivate.

We chatted and sipped for another hour. Drew understood. He trusted me; I knew that. And I had Drew's back; he knew that.

I didn't pay for the Pappy that night. We even stole a few beers to stay hydrated. We both knew that the announcement to the staff the next day was going to rock the rest of the team, so we talked about trying to get everybody prepped up early so that after the bomb blew up, we could clean up Chernobyl before customers arrived.

Nick, Barbra, and I made sure that the settlement had provided a generous severance for everyone who stayed until the end—one full month of pay, including tips for FOH. Drew received two years of salary for his dedication. He deserved every bit of it. We were also giving a three-month heads-up until we closed the doors. So, the explosion after the initial shock would be muted, slightly.

We had scheduled the release for four that afternoon because our staff would be together for lineup at that time. That way, they could hear it from us first, and we wouldn't violate the agreement. The nervous energy in the dining room peaked that Thursday as we tried to time our announcement exactly to the wire release. We knew it would only be a matter of minutes after the release when iPhones would start pinging with texts and tweets about the closing. The staff knew something was up. We had called people into the meeting who were off that day. And the kitchen staff rarely participated in line up because the purpose of line up was to bring the FOH up to speed on the menu and wines. It was obvious that something big was happening.

The group gathered around Nick and I. Barbara Cameron, our fantastic server, kept readjusting the knot of her gold tie and the collar of her black server jacket as she waited for us to speak. Our sous chef, Chef Paul, also known as Pauly, bounded into the group full of his usual energy.

Pauly's Jersey accent was audible as he gently nudged Barbara and asked in a whisper, "You know what's goin' on?"

Barbara shook her head, a few strands of her black hair falling across her pale, Irish features. She tucked the loose strands behind her ears.

I told them quickly and compassionately. A collective gasp was their response. Paul pat Barbara's arm gently with his free hand but held his shocked stare at us.

I let the news sink in with a decent pause. The severance and the long closure helped ease the blow.

A moment elapsed, and then Bryan Bergman, our red-headed jokester, and a beautiful person, spoke up. "Are you guys going to be okay?" he asked as he tried to blink back tears.

It wasn't at all what I expected for any of our staff to be worried about *us*. I was taken aback. The emotions were becoming harder to hide. But in retrospect, I knew that the entire staff had seen the wear and tear on Nick and me over the last two years of drama. They also saw the physical and emotional hits we took working the hours we worked day after day.

I assured Bryan that we would be fine.

As we walked away, there was an impromptu round of applause for us. Nick, Barbara, and I joined in to applaud the team – they deserved it, too. We were like family. We all walked the walk together every day. Nick was the hardest working guy on the floor at times, and they knew it. The kitchen team had the same view of me. Nick and I had that same view about every member of our staff. Everyone pulled their weight. It was a magical team wherein the sum was infinitely better than the individual parts. To me, the hardest thing about closing Cyrus was losing that team.

We were determined that the last three months at Cyrus would be fun. We had a blast. Our tables were in high demand, and we had a packed house every night. Countless investors and landlords approached us about reopening with them. We took it all in stride. We talked to a few. We politely declined the ones we knew to be a farce. But the truth is, I still didn't really know what I wanted at that time. I mean, I had something close to what I considered to be perfection at Cyrus, and it nearly killed me. Despite the awards, the best staff a chef could ask for, and even creating a more positive work environment, I wasn't happy; far from it. I needed time to figure out how I could be a chef and be healthy, both mentally and physically. That goal seemed almost impossible to me. I also knew I'd have to work toward facing and changing some of the brokenness of the industry, and I wasn't ready to tackle that yet. I wanted to enjoy the team and the next few months of being together and take care of our guests. That was the plan; go out like the rockstar team we were and enjoy every minute of it.

About a week before we closed, a potential investor reached out to do one last dinner at Cyrus. He wanted to bring a group of Silicon Valley people together for a night and discuss reopening Cyrus.

"It's white truffle season," I teased in response to his request, knowing he might be a fan.

His response gave me carte blanche to create the kind of epic meal my staff and I yearned to do before closing down.

Game on.

I reached out to Celine Lebaune from Gourmet Attitude in New York, my truffle magician who had never let me down.

"Celine, I don't care what it costs, but I need the biggest white truffle you can find me, one big, majestic piece. I have a dinner, and it needs to be epic."

Celine came through for me. A day before the dinner, the most gnarly truffle the size of a softball showed up at Cyrus. Price—ten grand. The aroma infected the entire kitchen as we unpacked it from the chilled shipping box. Yes, I admit that my iPhone came out, and we snapped photos. I had cooked a long time and had shaved a lot of truffles, but I'd never seen anything quite so impressive. I even called the local newspaper to invite them to take a shot as we would not likely see anything so grand again in Healdsburg.

The dinner was one for the books. The truffle was doing its job, and the interested investor was enthusiastic. After the white truffled French fry with individual fondue cheese course (think chili cheese fries in terms of how it's assembled, but flavored with truffles and expensive fondue cheese instead of chili and Cheez Whiz) launched the night into the stratosphere, I knew I had hit a homerun. And if I never cooked again, it would remain in my mind as a fantastic way to go out. We concluded with some of our miniature, maple-glazed crispy creams, as I knew that this particular potential investor loved them (valuable intel I had gathered from a previous dinner), and I waited for the reaction.

The potential investor led the entire table of twenty or so in a chant of, "More, more, more!"

Like I said, I had prepared for this. We had plenty of extras ready to go, and we fired off two or three more rounds. Gordon Gekko would have been proud. And I was happy. I had anticipated his needs and surpassed his expectations. I was cooking to make people happy again, and it felt great. That was a good first step in the right direction that night. The second step was letting myself dream again. I still didn't know what the future held for me, but at least I was starting to think about possibilities.

Over the next few weeks, Nick and I focused on saying goodbye to our staff. The reality and emotion of actually closing was finally settling in. Former staff stopped by to wish us good luck. The *Chronicle* did a countdown to the closing with a series of articles about our illustrious history. For the final day, Nick and I made a fake reservation sheet so that the staff would think that we had a full book of guests. But I didn't want guests there the last night. This restaurant had always been about the team at its core. I wanted to be with them and celebrate our incredible accomplishment.

When the team arrived, we had them help clean up a little for a few minutes. Then, pizza and champagne showed up. We had a nice party. Then, before we could get too drunk and destroy the furniture that wouldn't be ours in twelve hours, we moved to the B&B lounge, a place that had served as an important watering hole for us all. It takes a lot of beer to make a great restaurant.

As the party was inching towards debauchery in the best of ways, I eyed Lael that it was time. We had agreed to do an Irish exit. No way in hell I could say goodbye to everyone right there. My heart was heavy. We had the one and only taxi in Healdsburg standing by. We slipped towards the exit as Michael Jackson crooned "Billie Jean" from the juke box. I saw Chef Paul start to dance like no one was watching—but they all were. *How the fuck did he find a white glove? No way in hell this was planned.* I took one last look and slipped out the door and into the open taxi. Lael grabbed my hand, and I rested my head on her shoulder. We rode home in silence and in peace.

CHAPTER THIRTY-THREE

"Glycerine" (Acoustic) by Bush

Even though Cyrus was closed, I wasn't technically unemployed. I had the Healdsburg Bar and Grill under the direction of superstar chef John Hallgrimson, and I was keeping in touch with potential financial backers for a possible next restaurant down the road. Still, I had plenty of time on my hands for the first time since college. I made a list of summer goals: dinners with Lael; walks with dogs; no long pants or closed shoes for an entire summer. These feet needed to breathe after over twenty-five years of confinement, and I prefer shorts.

In a strong power grab for the 2013 Wife of the Year Award, Lael surprised me with a kegerator as a gift for closing Cyrus, and to assist in my enjoyment of spending time by the new pool that the Cyrus settlement had helped fund at our house. But the road to Hell is paved with good intentions, right? Something like that. My inability to do anything in moderation and a wicked case of gout caused our new appliance to be regifted after a few short months. It was a nice thought, though. Good on you, Lael. Bad on me.

We both realized I needed something to do besides tanning this melanoma-prone, white Irish body poolside and walking dogs in shorts. Lael had always wanted me to do a cooking show. She loved the competitions. But I had zero desire to compete on TV—ZERO. Cooking in the minute and making snap decisions about what to serve and how to serve it never appealed to my sensibilities. At Cyrus, it would take me weeks to change a menu item. We would think about an idea for a while, let it percolate, and then slowly start to test versions of it. We never served it to a paying guest (no paying guinea pigs, thank you) until we had worked out the kinks and were sure it was up to par. Thus, the idea of being told what to cook, or being given a vague riddle of an idea, and then being told I had thirty minutes to make it happen and serve it seemed unreal and intimidating. Also, the thought of being judged by a group of people who may or may not be qualified (just like my aversion to Yelp reviewers), and who would be directed by a television crew whose main goal would be to get good ratings as opposed to intellectually discussing the food or teaching something about cooking to the audience. No thanks.

I'm not against all cooking shows. Julia Child and Jacques Pepin on PBS in the 1980s and 1990s clearly cared about furthering the culinary landscape in America. They taught real cooking skills to the American viewers. There was great value in that. I don't understand how the television executives went from broadcasting Julia and Jacques teaching cooking to Mario Batali in shorts and Crocs. There are now aspiring chefs who believe that they can skip actually learning the skill of cooking if they just pass the audition test for *Hell's Kitchen* and get to the finale while Gordon Ramsey berates and belittles them. Ratings, you know.

Sometimes I fail to see the value in modern cooking shows. I also feel that some of these shows ignore the hard work and thoughtfulness of what we do in the kitchens. Like an over-reduced stock, some of the shows seem too intense, too bitter, and not at all healthy. The idea that modern cooking shows mimic the realities of what happens in professional kitchens is offensive.

But I must admit that many good things have come from the production of this new generation of cooking shows. More farmer's markets popped up around the country. People who had previously only had access to iceberg salads with a choice of ranch, Russian, or Italian at their local restaurants suddenly had arugula and thin crust pizzas on their local menus. People began to venture out from their hibernations of culinary comfort. They also started to take note of where their food was coming from. Many charities also benefited from the culinary television boom. Celebrity chef competition shows not only advertised for celebrity charities, but they gave them money, too. A lot of good was coming from these shows.

The *Top Chef* phenomenon landed in our homes via the Bravo television network at the right time. The interest in everything cooking was rising astronomically. The idea of pitting young, budding cooks against each other in organized challenges that tested their cooking skills and entertained as well was a brilliant idea by The Magical Elves Production Company. No way they could have foreseen the market they had just uncorked; but *bravo* to them.

I had made numerous appearances on many shows over the years, but always from a safe role as a guest judge. I had never agreed to be a contestant when asked. I had neither the ability nor the desire to step away from Cyrus for the three straight weeks of filming required. It was simply out of the question. But when those Magical Elves approached me, I did have time.

I was invited to compete on *Top Chef Masters,* a slightly more refined version of *Top Chef* for already established chefs.

I think Lael's desire to ship me off to some kind of summer camp had a direct influence on my decision to finally give it a try, but I also had a charity to represent—Green Dog Rescue Project. Green Dog was in its fledgling stage and could definitely use the extra money and exposure. Lael's gentle prods finally pushed me out of my comfort zone enough to say yes. She must have known something I didn't; she always does.

I didn't expect to win. I had culinary confidence but also a healthy dose of television limitations. The show allotted thirty minutes to the chefs to think of a dish, prep it, and then serve it.

The start of a quickfire challenge on the show began just like any race with the announcement. "Your time starts NOW!" (Emphasis added to mimic the firing of a starting gun.)

The chefs would then scurry like bleeding rabbits to grab whatever ingredients they could before the other contestants got them. Then, they'd race to gather their tools and prepare their dishes at a feverish pace. I wouldn't be able to function like that on the show. I had some significant physical limitations. First, ever since the brain surgery, I haven't been able to run. Some days, I can't even walk straight. I knew I didn't have a chance to get my choice of ingredients for any challenge on the show. I also wouldn't be able to work as fast as the other contestants.

During the filming of my introduction interview, the producer, Wade Sheeler, asked me why I thought I would win *Top Chef Masters*.

"Oh, I don't think I will," I said far too honestly. "I don't cook like this, so I'm just hoping I don't go home first, and I can win a few bucks for the pups."

Wade replied that we might need to shoot that question again. I could tell that my honesty was getting in the way of his job.

"Ask me again," I offered.

"Rolling!" Wade called out.

"Luck of the Irish, of course," I said to the cameras.

The first week was brutal. I wanted to quit many times. I was also struggling with my ego more than ever, a struggle which manifested in the judging of my dishes by the guest celebrity judges they brought in to inject a little, well, celebrity appeal, into the show. I guess co-contestant and friend Sang Yoon and I weren't enough to push the Nielsens.

I have no problem with anyone having an opinion about a dish I make, especially a paying guest. Celebrity or not, everyone is entitled to say whether or not they like something and give reasons why. The main judges, Ruth Reichl and Gail Simmons, were chefs, food writers, and critics with experience. If Gail Simmons didn't like my dish, I knew she was being honest and had the credibility to back up her criticism. I could disagree with her, but I wouldn't question her ability or her intentions. What I have no stomach for, whatsoever, is someone who is not technically qualified to offer a technical critique, but who attempts to give such a critique anyway instead of just saying whether or not he or she liked how the dish tasted to him or her. That was everything I hated about Yelp reviews. When those unqualified guest judges give those technical critiques with an air of superiority, it just burned me.

Thus, when LA radio DJ Jason Bentley announced that I "obviously didn't understand the challenge," I may have lost it a little. The challenge Bentley judged was the Reinvent Curry Challenge. The other chefs were blown away by the coconut water, curry-infused consommé with poached sole. It *was* phenomenal; that's a technical fact as opposed to opinion, by the way. Sorry, I couldn't help myself.

"Actually, Bentley," I said with cameras rolling, "it's painfully obvious that you don't understand what a curry is."

Bentley went limp, his expression a mixture of embarrassment and rage. The host, Curtis Stone, shifted uncomfortably as his eyes darted from me to Bentley. Bryan Voltaggio (a competing chef on the show who was standing next to me) kicked me, a well-meaning gesture urging me to shut up. He didn't want me to piss off anyone and get kicked out. But I was unplugged and couldn't stop.

I then gave the celebrity DJ a rapid-fire dissertation of what went into a curry. As Bryan continued kicking me, I presented a point-by-point rundown of what was in my dish and how it worked. Then, I went for the kill. You should know me well enough by now to have seen this coming.

"You probably shouldn't come on a cooking show if you're going to say stupid things," I stated.

On another day and another challenge, the geriatric cast of *Days of Our Lives* told Odette Fada that her egg yolk ravioli was not good, the yolk was too runny, and it was cold. Then, in a magnificent display of ignorance, they said that Odette's dish was "just weird."

I rolled my eyes and sighed loud enough for all to hear. First of all, for Odette to pull off a handmade ravioli stuffed with an egg yolk in the time allowed was nothing short of miraculous. I tasted it, and it was perfect. I can guess that, had she puréed the entire dish and spoon-fed it to the soap stars, they would have been a little more comfortable with it, since most of them might not have been able to chew due to their Botox injections. But the audacity of the statement that it was *weird* showed how out of their league the soap stars were. Egg yolk ravioli is a brilliant dish that many Italian chefs have plated over the years in imitation of Odette's vision. So, it's not weird by any definition. The cold comment was equally asinine. All of the food was always cold on the set. The food cannot be served upon its completion because after filming the cooking process, the next shoot must set up before the judges can taste the food. Judges and contestants are told to just not worry about the temperature, and that temperature should not be taken into consideration. The *Days of Our Lives* cast obviously didn't get that memo, or maybe the print was just too small.

Odette stood there and took their inept criticism silently. But I couldn't let it stand. I wanted to let Odette know that I got it. It was awesome, and so was she. So, when it was my turn to defend my dish, I instead used my time to give them a little history of the ravioli dish that Odette had presented and let them know as unsubtly as possible what I thought of their opinions.

"Odette's dish is brilliant, and it was executed perfectly," I began. "The fact that you thought it was weird just shows that you all are way out of your league. You don't have the sophisticated palate to judge her."

Another judge, a food critic from a Los Angeles magazine, got all huffy and said, "I have a sophisticated palate, and I didn't like it either."

I admit that I probably rolled my eyes at her, too, before responding, "I haven't met a food critic that didn't truly believe they had a sophisticated palate, but most are wrong." Yeah, I was in a special place at that time.

If you watch season five of *Top Chef Masters*, you won't see the exchanges with Bentley or with the *Days of Our Lives* cast. They were edited out. Shocking, I know.

The night after the ravioli incident, I called Lael and said I was coming home. I was tired, I missed the dogs, and I was fed up with the bullshit.

Lael listened patiently, and then said, "You aren't coming home yet. You can do this. You're doing it for the pups. Promise me one more day. Then, you can leave if you really want."

I spent the next few hours lying awake and wondering why I felt so angry and so tired. I knew that a lot of it had to do with my ego and my need for my work and the work of all chefs and kitchen staff to be appreciated and respected. But I didn't know how to stop being so damn needy. Here I was again, facing the same issues of affirmation that I had at Bauer's Four-Star Dinner. Why couldn't I just relax and have fun with the show? Why did the idiots bother me so much? I had promised Lael another day. I knew that I could either spend that day pissed off, or I could spend the day just cooking like no one was watching, letting the comments roll off my back, and trying to have fun with the other chefs. I made the choice Lael had hoped I'd make; I decided to let all that anger and frustration go. I decided to stop being so damn needy, let go of some of my ego (baby steps, people), and just stop taking myself so seriously. It was only one day. I resolved to do it.

I walked onto the set the next day a different person. I found the humor in the celebrity absurdity. I let my ego slip to the back of my brain and just enjoyed cooking, the hard-working and funny chefs, and the amazing crew on the show. I chose to appreciate the silly challenges and the good products we were given. I got over myself and lived in the moment for a change. And it was glorious.

The Quickfire Challenge presented to me in my newly attained positive state was to cook a dish based on our celebrity guest judge's favorite romantic comedy, *Midnight in Paris*. Our celebrity judge for that episode was none other than Mindy Kaling, comedian, writer, producer, and star of *The Mindy Project*. True confession. I had no idea what the show was about, but I did recognize her. I had also never seen *Midnight in Paris*, but I zeroed in on three things: late night; French food; romantic. Ivy League, baby.

I had a plan for the day's challenge. Instead of focusing on the frustration of not being able to outrun (or to run at all) the other chefs to the food room to get my pick of ingredients, I decided to remember my training and begin the challenge with the basis of all kitchen success: *Mise en Place,* everything in its place. The system had been beaten into me at Lespinasse. I'd set up my station first, and it would save me time later.

The single most consistent question I am asked about my time on *Top Chef Masters* is, "Was the cooking real?"

Yes, the cooking was very real in regard to the time the viewers saw, and the time chefs got to cook. There were no pauses once the clock starts ticking. There were no secret dishes being pulled out of the oven by an imaginary Oompla Loompa cooking crew. It was thirty minutes of blood, sweat, and tears before the command, "Knives down."

"Your time starts now!" the host hollered.

As the other chefs sprinted to the refrigerator, I calmly set up my station with cutting boards, towels, knives, seasoning, water to clean, and so on. Next, as my co-contestants were still fighting over ingredients in a huddled mass in the food room, I worked backward and gathered my plates. When I finally limped back to the food area, the other chefs were gone. They were then back in the main kitchen fighting for pots and pans, feverishly chopping, and trying to decide what they were going to actually make with the bounty of ingredients they'd scored. I, on the other hand, was looking at a refrigerator with almost no choices; there was pretty much nothing left but eggs. *Hmm; okay, eggs it is.*

If you asked me for an idea for a sexy, late-night dish to cook for a date, scrambled eggs would come to mind right away. I love eggs myself; most chefs do. There's a sensual texture to perfectly soft scrambled eggs. It really was an ideal fit for this romantic date Mindy and I were supposedly on. What better way to win the adoring love of your date than spooning meltingly luxurious, buttery silken eggs into her mouth? My farm fresh eggs also would not take very long to cook. *Bonus!* I realized that I could still win this thing, even with my slow limp. *Slow and steady wins the race.*

Before I left the food room, I scanned the shelves one last time and spotted a small tin of caviar that had been overlooked. Caviar and scrambled eggs; this was almost too easy. My dish was appropriate for the task at hand, easy to make, and delicious. I had Paris with the caviar and midnight with the scrambled eggs. *What about the comedy part?* I thought. *I mean, who wants a date who takes himself too seriously? And who doesn't love French fries?* I'd just spotted the potatoes on the table next to me. Scrambled eggs with fries and caviar. *Goddamn, this came together well!*

I headed back to my station and set about my tasks in order of importance. The fries would take the longest, so I heated up a small pot of water and a small pot of oil. French fries may seem like an easy thing to most casual observers, but to make really good ones, you need to respect the starch of the potato. It takes three separate cooking and cooling sessions to make a perfectly crunchy, golden-brown on the outside, and creamy, puffy, soft on the inside fry. Most French fries you get in restaurants have been precooked by a company and then frozen. I am here to tell you that's a good thing. For many reasons, those commercially produced fries create a more consistent product in an efficient way. The end product is usually better. I would have killed for some frozen fries for Mindy that day.

When my fries were chilling, I very slowly scrambled my eggs with a fair amount of butter, barely stirring to create the best mouthfeel possible. I had ten minutes to go, and I was going to use almost every second to my advantage. Two minutes out, as my eggs were starting to set, I dropped my fries in the fat for their final fry to crispy golden perfection. I sliced some chives razor thin so the fresh, bulby taste and smell would contradict the rich, creamy eggs and caviar in the best of ways. As I pulled out my fries and patted them down a little to absorb the excess oil, my eggs were perfecting themselves in the pan—soft, creamy, and moist. I then gently spooned the eggs onto the plate and generously mounded way too much of the caviar on top. Greed, in that case, was good. Plus, it was a date, and I needed to impress. A little sprinkle of the chives and a scattering of French fries completed the task.

Five grand to Green Dog Rescue Project! Thank you very much, Ms. Kaling!

I ended up winning the entire show, and with that win came one hundred and twenty grand for Green Dog Rescue Project. I teared up when I thought about what that would do for my fledgling charity. Also, the exposure for the charity and our message was invaluable. Beyond helping the pups, the experience of being on the show helped me. It taught me how I needed to get over myself in order to stop being so angry. I also needed an experience to help me realize that I could still win despite my post-brain surgery. Good health might look a little different on me, but I could work with where I was at. Yeah, Lael knew exactly what she was doing when she urged me to go on that cooking show. It was never really about the cooking, was it? *Bravo.*

CHAPTER THIRTY-FOUR

"Sympathy"
by The Goo Goo Dolls

"You need an agent," Stan stated.

I'd just gotten back from filming the final episode of *Top Chef Masters*. Stan knew before I did that the show would give me even more culinary leverage.

"Really?" I asked.

Stan wasn't the first person to suggest that I obtain an agent. I laughed it off at first. *I cook dinner. I don't need an agent. I don't want to be a TV personality.* But Stan solidified my suspicion that I should indeed seek out representation. I had learned that it's important to understand what I don't know. I may very well be the smartest person in the room on a topic sometimes (like how to cook red wine risotto), but no way in hell am I the smartest person on every topic. I'd had family and Stan give me counsel for as long as I could remember, but this was different. I needed someone with experience in TV, advertising, and social media.

Even though I knew to follow the advice from Stan and other friends, it was hard for me to do. I did the show to raise money for charity, not to put myself under Hollywood lights. I had no expectation of opportunities after *Top Chef Masters*. I figured that if something else did come up, then I would just use the appropriate lawyers as I always had. The whole idea of representation for a chef had just seemed counterintuitive. Despite my ambivalence, I had to admit that TV and media could be another source of leverage if I approached it the right way.

So, I took a few meetings in Los Angeles with three of the most chef-appropriate agents suggested to me by friends in the business. The lobbies at the agencies were pretty cool with their spit-polished marble, shiny poured concrete, and tons of glass shooting up high into the LA sky. But the allure always ended in the lobby for me. The life-size photos of Guy Fieri, Mario Batali, and Gordon Ramsay on display throughout the offices that I passed as I was escorted to the meetings seemed too ostentatious for my lower profile. The agency meetings were exactly what I had feared—discussions about ancillary opportunities, mass-marketing strategies, and branding.

My brand, I thought, *is Doug: I drive a truck, I cook dinner, I play with dogs, I'm sarcastic, and I don't want to be in this meeting any longer.*

I know the agents I met with didn't like me, and it was mutual. No way in hell I was going to work with them. I could read it on their faces; they saw no value in me either. For them, I was, perhaps, too heavy, not edgy enough, or too nice. Each encounter reminded me of the one time I went on a blind date in Manhattan. The girl suggested coffee at ten at night for the meeting. *Coffee? Do they serve any booze?* We met, had nothing in common, and realized that we had zero attraction to each other just six minutes into it.

"No need to drag this out any longer," I had told her.

Maybe it's me being a little naïve, but I thought she appreciated the mercy killing, too.

I felt the same way at the last agent meeting I had scheduled. I couldn't see the point any longer, and I didn't want to waste another minute I would definitely never get back.

"Thanks," I said as politely as possible as I stood. "I appreciate your time."

I think the room was slightly stunned by my candidness but was relieved by my departure. I felt gross after that initial meeting just as I had after every other meeting I had taken. Each left me with a desire to sit on the ground in a park and just touch dirt, or rocks, or anything that was real. I also kind of wanted a shower.

After my last agency meeting, I returned to my hotel room and called Jordan Bromley, Stan's youngest child whom I had known since his birth. Little Jordie was now an entertainment lawyer and partner at one of the biggest law firms in LA. He laughed when I recounted my day.

"Yeah, that sounds right," Jordan offered. "They're a bunch of dip shits for the most part. But hey, you should meet my friends Randy and Harriet. They aren't agents. They're managers of talent, and they have one other chef. They're always looking for good people. Do you like *American Idol*?"

"Yeah, I love it actually. Why?"

"Randy is Randy Jackson from *American Idol*. He's great. You'll love him. He and Harriet Sternberg represent some music acts I work with. Harriet also has an incredible history in the music business. She's worked with Kenny Rogers, Lionel Richie, the 'We Are the World' project, and the list goes on and on. We've gotten to know each other really well over the years, and they're really good people."

"What would they want with me?" I blurted.

"Who knows?" he replied in his best hipster tone. "But why not meet them? You're in LA, after all."

We met at the Montage, a hotel in LA. It was very white—white walls, white ceilings, white floors, and white tables to furnish the place. Dressed in a suit and tie, I met Jordan first, and he explained that Randy and Harriet might not want to stay long, and that I shouldn't be offended. I had no expectations. I found it funny that I was meeting Randy Jackson and his illustrious partner about a very remote possibility of working together.

Randy sauntered in in style, clad in lots of bling and brand new, sharp sneakers. The man positively beamed. He smiled wide, flashing his extremely bright pearly whites, and stopped to shake hands with all who approached him. He even gave a hug here and there, and then greeted the staff who seemed to know him. His energy was infectious. Harriet demurred behind him, to his side, or in front when necessary. She was always smiling, but she never took the lead.

About an hour into our meeting, Jordan got up and said he had to leave for another meeting. Randy, Harriet, and I sat together for another two hours. We talked about dreams and ideas.

"If you were in a commercial, what company would it be for and why?" Harriet asked.

"Ford Trucks, for sure," I replied. "Born and raised in Detroit, and I've never driven anything else. I've opened every restaurant with a Ford, driven seven of my dogs in Fords, and I still have my F150 now with over two-hundred-thousand miles on it. Ford would be a natural for me."

Can I even see myself doing a commercial? I wondered.

"We know Ford," Randy responded. "They're a sponsor of *American Idol*. We should talk to them, Harriet."

I indulged in a daydream for a second that I could get a new truck out of a deal with Ford. I didn't need one at the time. I was still attached to the F150 I had because I had bought it after my dad died with some money he left me. But the thought was exciting.

"So, we should explain that if we do business together, we don't work like agents," Harriet said.

Harriet went on to explain that an agent's job is to work their many clients to earn as much as possible from every possible opportunity.

"Instead," Harriet continued, "we work to help you make your dreams come true. We help you shape your image to achieve your goals. We bring ideas to you, but if you aren't comfortable with any of those ideas, then we don't discuss it further. We advise you about how to create opportunities that you are comfortable with. For example, I know you're into rescuing dogs. So, we could explore working with a brand of dog food if you want."

We've been working together ever since. They have negotiated top-notch deals for me with Dell, Pete's Coffee, Pepsi, and Stacy's Pita Chips. Harriet has become one of my closest friends. We text and retweet each other multiple times a day, especially about politics. But it goes deeper. I don't know if many days have gone by that we haven't communicated. I'm not sure what to make of my partnership with those two wonderful people. They are managers and friends, and I cherish their counsel.

And maybe we'll score a Ford commercial someday. Or a tire company—but not Michelin.

CHAPTER THIRTY-FIVE

"Old Man" (Live)
by Neil Young

As I was applying SPF 900 lotion to my white, Irish, melanoma magnet of a body one late summer day, my phone rang.

"Barbara Banke would like to speak with you about Cyrus," the assistant stated through the phone. "Would you like to have coffee with her?"

When certain people want to talk to you, you just do it, no questions asked. Barbara Banke is the leader of Jackson Family Wines. She and her late husband, Jess Jackson, built one of the world's greatest wine and real estate businesses. In Sonoma County, there is no bigger fish than Barbara Banke, and her pond extends across the world.

"Of course," I replied without hesitation.

It's taken me a while, but I've had to learn to not be biased against extremely wealthy people. Neither jealousy nor bitterness drove my prejudice. I just believed that there were a disproportionate percentage of assholes in the really wealthy segment of the population. My time in swanky New York City restaurants and Napa certainly perpetuated my negative view of people with deep pockets, but the prejudice really developed from my childhood observations of my dad and Aunt Maureen in their reactions to the rich people they encountered.

Dad and Aunt Mo idolized wealthy people for only that attribute, and that disturbed me. They would describe a wealthy person with an air of deference and awe as someone who owned the entire city of Scottsdale or who was the biggest landowner in all of Michigan. These statements took the place of any commentary about the individual's personality or level of kindness. Dad and Aunt Maureen were themselves successful individuals. Although they had grown up dirt poor, they worked their way up and captured the American Dream for themselves. So, even though their fascination with wealth was understandable given their background, I could never understand why they tolerated so many assholes just because of money and status. In a weird way, my dad and aunt wanted rich people to like them more than they should have. Thus, I developed a bit of a prejudice against the rich.

There's an irony in this that can't be overlooked. It's virtually impossible to be in the high-end restaurant business without some extremely wealthy people lending some assistance and being patrons. Rich people have money and look for places to invest, and rich people can afford great food and wine. Investing in the restaurant business can be a natural temptation for anyone with means who loves great food. And, as I explained earlier, the restaurant business is notoriously risky, so banks are appropriately skittish about restaurant investing. So, wealthy people are really the only people who can afford the risk. So, if you are in my shoes looking for investors, it's a Hobson's choice. The truth is, money doesn't buy happiness, but it *does* buy some freedom.

Barbara Banke helped me to shed my prejudice against the very rich. I never had a negative impression of her. From my first months in Sonoma County, it was obvious how important Barbara was to the business community. Maybe my good impression of Barbara stemmed from the observation that she never took over a room without reason. Maybe the positive vibe was because every employee of Barbara's that I'd ever met said only wonderful things about her and about how they were genuinely happy to work with her. Maybe I thought so well of her because she once showed me the locket her kids gave her for a present that was most likely intended to hold their pictures, but, instead, she proudly filled it with pictures of her two cherished labs. Yeah, that one went a long way in my book. Maybe it was just because she was really easy to talk to. With Barbara, I always felt I was dealing with a genuine person who cared about community, family, people, business, and animals. She didn't use her wealth to dominate others. Money didn't define her. She didn't need it. Barbara was and is best defined as a strong businesswoman with a big heart and a desire to contribute to her community. I said it before, and I'll say it again, we need more women in this business, and in all businesses actually. Barbara helped me to realize that the jerks my dad and Aunt Mo interacted with were just that—jerks. Their awful behavior would have defined them regardless of the amount of money they had. I'm sure the same is true of the Napa bullies and others of that ilk I had encountered.

So, when Barbara's assistant suggested I have coffee with her boss, even though I had no desire to talk Cyrus rebirth yet, I accepted because I liked Barbara, because I respected her, and because she asked. I wondered who would pay. I mean, she was a billionaire and all. You should get some benefits from rich friends, right?

Barbara was on time for our coffee date at The Flying Goat in Healdsburg. I immediately liked her even more. Then, she said something that changed everything for me.

"I just want you to know that my family and I think Cyrus was really important for Sonoma County," she began. "We already miss you, and whatever we can do to help you come back to Sonoma County, we will assist you. Just ask."

I was floored. I didn't expect that. I didn't expect anything, really. But this person, sipping a latte, who was arguably the most important fixture in Sonoma County, was telling me that our little fifty-six-seat restaurant was important to her and to Sonoma. At that moment in the Flying Goat, Barbara Banke believed in me way more than I believed in myself. I hadn't grasped that our restaurant had meant so much to the people around us in the community. I choked back some emotion before I was able to speak.

I confided in her that I really wasn't sure what I was going to do or what I had the energy for. She was wise and patient enough to allow me to whine for a little bit. She listened like a sage, responded that she wanted me to reopen, and repeated her offer to help.

"Money, land, guidance with the county . . . just ask," she repeated. "Cyrus closed too soon, and Sonoma needs it back." She gently pushed a little and asked me to tell her how I would reinvent Cyrus if I did it again. I flashed back to a conversation many years ago with Traci Des Jardins when I first politely declined her job offer. Traci didn't beg me to take the job on her second and third attempt. She didn't try and bully me. She spoke calmly and confidently and pointed out why it was a good idea to work with her. Barbara had taken the same brilliant, gentle, and genuine approach. She was letting me in on a secret. I should do Cyrus again, I was going to do Cyrus again, and she just needed to convince me of the future reality. Boys need more help a lot of the time.

I think Barbara would have been content to have me reopen Cyrus just as it had been, but in a different location, as long as it was in Sonoma County. But I wanted to take it to the next level and recreate a new and improved Cyrus smack dab in the magical vineyards of Sonoma County. Our first eight years of operating, minus the lawsuits and fighting with landlords, were nothing short of a two-way love fest. Sonoma County loved having us, and we loved working and living here. It would have been a betrayal of trust to export Cyrus to any other place, and now I knew that Barbara Banke shared those feelings with me about Cyrus.

I decided to let it rip and tell her the idea that had been incubating for a few years. There was something comforting, real, and safe about her approach. She helped me to allow myself to open up.

"It'll be on a hill, in Alexander Valley and floating over the vines, and it will be modern looking and gorgeous."

I also emphasized that I wanted Cyrus to remain rooted in the tenets of hospitality, style, and substance. The new Cyrus (dubbed Cyrus 2.0), though offering a culinary experience that would push the envelope in terms of innovation and creativity, needed to be familiar enough that people wouldn't be uncomfortable or challenged too much, and the bar had to remain high in terms of taking care of the guests. Thanks to Stan's constant coaching and critiques over the years, these were principles Nick and I had lived by.

The first Cyrus was all of the great things I had seen in other restaurants over the course of my studies and career with my spin on it. The flavors and the little flourishes were mine, but the champagne cart, the mini breads, and the candies at the end were all things that had been done before in concept.

"The new creation," I said, "well, it's this unique idea I've been incubating in my mind for years, ever since my time in Kyoto."

"Go ahead," Barbara encouraged. "If our family can help in any way, we will."

In that moment, I went for it. Why not? How many times do you get to have someone want to listen to your crazy dreams and actually offer to help you achieve them? This was a first for this scrappy kid from Dearborn, so I chose to swing and not worry about sounding like a wacky artist.

"I want to take people on an actual dining journey instead of just another four-hour dinner. Twelve people at a time. Three seatings. Thirty-six people a night."

Barbara's raised eyebrows and slight grin further fueled my pitch; she was intrigued.

I explained that, in my mind, the current spate of luxury restaurants with multiple courses, four-hour meals served to guests remaining seated at the same table all evening had become somewhat stupefying and overwhelming for guests. Resistance was slowly growing to the traditional tasting menu format. Guests seemed to be saying, *been there done that*. That reality dovetailed with my memories of traditional Kaiseki dining that I fell in love with during my time in Kyoto, and my vision was born. In Kyoto, I would spend the entire evening in one beautiful room, despite being told about other gorgeous rooms in the restaurant furnished with unique art that I would never see because they were occupied by other patrons that evening. *Why even tell me?* I thought. The obvious evolution to me would be to create a *journey* for the meal.

"The idea is actually pretty simple," I continued. "It's based on how we welcome people into our homes and create an environment that moves them smoothly through an evening. Every so often, we offer our guests new stimulation via moving to a new room or having a new encounter, but it is these connected events that will form a single, unique journey. Instead of testing endurance with hours spent at the same table, Cyrus will have guests checking their watches and marveling at how quickly the evening has flown by."

Barbara nodded, still smiling. I realized that I wasn't delivering a sales pitch; I was storytelling, and this one was personal.

"Tell me about the different parts of the journey," she said, as our coffees got cold.

"Each part of the journey is related to the original Cyrus experience," I began, "but we're breaking ground with the journey concept. Others will mimic it down the road, but I'll own the concept – all my own IP, baby. The meal will begin very much like an evening of entertainment at home with a warm welcome and bites and sips in the Bubbles Room. Guests will take in breathtaking views of surrounding vineyards and stunning garden landscapes. The scene in the Bubbles Room will unfold under the magical lighting of the early evening, Alexander Valley skies. The first five tastes guests receive will highlight the five taste categories: sweet, sour, salty, bitter, and umami, a detail reminiscent of the first Cyrus.

"Following this reception, the seating of twelve will move to The Kitchen Table where they will have an interactive experience looking on as their next few courses are prepared directly in front of them. Designed like a high-end sushi counter, this room will invoke, through its architecture and design, an almost spiritual reverence for the purity of the food. This portion of the meal will feature a pristine bounty of seafood as well as raw preparations of vegetables from local gardens.

"Next, the group will move to a more traditional dining space, and each party will have their own table for their final savory courses. This dining room will be designed to give every guest a stunning view of the scenery and mimic the sensation of floating above the Alexander Valley vines. There will be room for all guests to be seated at the same time, creating the gentle buzz of a refined restaurant.

"After a small dessert is served in the Dining Room, the guests will be escorted to a room inspired by both Willy Wonka and The Michelin Man . . . if they had a baby. As guests approach the room, they may be initially underwhelmed, just as Mr. Wonka's golden ticket winners were, but that feeling will dissipate quickly as they pass through a partition in a flowing wall of chocolate. Then, with the generous spirit of a traditional *mignardise* presentation, little delectable chocolate treats will wondrously appear as guests move along the path towards the exit lounge. The chocolates will reinforce the full loop of the dining journey, echoing the welcoming *canapés* five tastes—sweet, sour, salty, bitter and umami.

"Upon leaving the Chocolate Room, our patrons will be invited to linger in the exit lounge, enjoy their chocolate bites, sip on an after-dinner drink, or simply gaze at the clear sky through the open roof of the lounge while sitting by a warm fire."

"That's it?" Barbara joked jovially. She seemed to get it. Or at least she wanted me to strive for this dream.

"Nope, there's more," I told her. "That was the artist side, the rest is the business side and the social conscience side."

"Do tell," she said as she jumped back into her latte.

"I want to reinvent the staffing model."

I explained how I had been frustrated by the lack of innovation in my industry in terms of creating a long-term staffing model that supported careers and paid people a decent living wage versus the short-term model we had all been using. The current norm was a deeply frustrating cycle with high turnover, significant disparity between the back and front of house, and an inability to create long-term stability for both employees and businesses.

"Any industry person will tell you," I began, "that the high rate of turnover in restaurant staff is a problem. Our industry is just rife with reasons for our staffs to not stay long. The industry doesn't pay enough. Restaurant workers can't make ends meet. Most can't afford health insurance, let alone incidentals beyond rent, food, and basic clothing. The shitty schedules add up over time and instill resentment. Remember that restaurants are always open on nights, weekends, and holidays. You can only miss so many family holidays, birthdays, and weddings before the anger digs in deep. Sick days aren't a thing. It took a brain tumor to get me to go to a doctor, and even then, I scheduled that appointment on a day off. Vacation and retirement are virtually nonexistent. The whole industry is a breeding ground for dysfunction and unhealthy lifestyles.

"The solution to the high rate of turnover," I continued, "is to give all employees a true living wage. If you really want to build a great business, you don't look at the cheapest way to do it. If you pick the cheapest stove and refrigeration out there, I promise you it will cost more down the road in replacements and repairs. Labor is, by far and away, the biggest investment in the restaurant business, and it costs way too much when turnover is high. We need to pay staff enough to have a good, healthy lifestyle so that they want to stick around for the long run."

"Makes sense," Barbara said.

"Next," I continued, "we've got to even the playing field for all of the staff. In a typical high-end restaurant, there is often a 100 percent or greater difference in earnings between a server and a cook. It's not uncommon for a top-level waiter to make eighty thousand to one hundred thousand per year, while a line cook, at best, will top out at forty thousand. This disparity can be traced directly to our system of tipping and the laws that help shape it. There just isn't any logical justification to tip one segment of the staff and not the other. It's purely tradition, and a stupid one at that. It's also worth questioning why it's even legal for waiters or waitresses to work without knowing whether they will get the bulk of their income in any given shift. In practice, which depends more on the generosity of the customers than on their work. Please understand that I don't begrudge servers their money, by the way. I would just like to see *all* of the staff get to the seventy-to-eighty thousand range."

"And how would you do that?" Barbara asked.

I couldn't help but grin. I was then, and am now as I write, proud of my plan. "We cut our staffing needs in half by combining the roles of back and front of house employees. We'll cross-train the staff for all positions. Then, even though our labor cost will remain the same, we can pay each member of our staff roughly double what we used to pay. My goal is a seventy-five-thousand-dollar salary to start. They'll get that living wage, and the turnover rate will drop. *And* the cross-training will enable us to accommodate sick days and leaves of absence for childbirth and family emergencies, a practice that is standard in other industries. Staff can also rotate holidays. Because everyone will be able to cover for several positions, we will be able to allow people to attend those family weddings and birthdays, too. Then, I want to close for three weeks each year—two weeks in the slow, winter season of Sonoma County, and one week during the summer so parents can spend a week with their kids during school break."

"You believe this is possible?" Barbara asked.

I don't think she expected that I wanted to make the world a better place, too. But I knew that her business was a leader in social conscience, so I suspected she was just checking out whether I had thought through this lofty goal.

"Absolutely," I stated firmly. "You have to make some changes, find efficiencies, make use of technology, and possibly cut out steps of service. But with the right thinking, it can be done. And with Cyrus being brand new and highly visible, I want to establish a better model for the industry and inspire a long-term effect on employee sustainability in the restaurant business globally."

Barbara seemed jazzed about all of it. I let her know once again that this model would require a higher initial investment in training, but that would eventually yield lower overall labor costs and higher long-term profits.

Barbara's encouragement firmly planted the seeds in my mind that I should be open to trying it again—the whole shebang—the four-star dream, version 2.0. That one conversation touched me deeply. Other investors had approached me, but Barbara spoke on behalf of our community, those I most wanted to serve. (Barbara, if I haven't properly thanked you yet, please accept my gratitude now.)

By the way, I paid for both of our coffees that morning. I felt guilty for thinking I could milk a friend for a free coffee. As we both headed to our trucks, I thought again about how lucky I was to have certain people in my life who took the time to offer their guidance and their help.

CHAPTER THIRTY-SIX

"House of Gold" by Twenty One Pilots

It was just days later when I again hopped into my beloved F150, recently outfitted with Bluetooth capability, and I received a series of phone calls that made me realize that I had even more help than I thought to pursue my next Cyrus. Cash, Finny, and I were on our way to Green Dog Rescue to play with our best buddy, Jakey. When the first call rang through, I proudly spoke up to the visor (Bluetooth made me feel legit) and fumbled with the volume (yeah, hands free).

"Hi, Doug." It was Barbara Gordon, my partner, my lawyer, and my friend from Cyrus. "Greg Lane called." Greg Lane was Bill Foley's fix-it man. Greg wanted my advice on how to deal with a sensitive situation. I told her to let Greg know we had nothing. I had some doggies to play with. I hung up.

My phone rang again just minutes later. This time, it was the assistant to Sandy Weill, former chairman of Citigroup.

"Could you have lunch with Sandy? He really wants to chat about Cyrus at Weill Hall- Sonoma State again."

I liked Sandy and his wife, Joan. He treated her like gold, and she doted on him. They were gracious, hospitable, and easy to talk to. And, like Barbara Banke, they believed in what we did at Cyrus and how important it was to Sonoma County. Sandy was determined for us to reopen Cyrus at his namesake project. I would have lunch with him anytime. He was also a Cornell guy. But I didn't answer yet. Jakey needed me more than Sandy did right then, and I'd decided that if I was going to move forward with another restaurant, I was going to finally do so with some balance in my life. I resisted the strong urge to respond immediately and proudly stuck with my morning plan of going to Green Dog. I'd call back later.

Within a few minutes, the phone rang again. I recognized the area code number. It was Barbara Banke's assistant following up after our coffee meeting.

"Hi Douglas. Would you like to see a few of the Jackson wine properties for a potential Cyrus location?"

Of course I would. But I'd tell them yes later. Jakey the dog needed me, and the truth is, I needed him, too.

Just minutes after I hung up with Barbara Banke's assistant, Barbara Gordon called me again. I relayed to her my two previous calls.

"What's up now?" I asked.

"Sean Parker's attorney, Steve Wolff, called to say that Sean wants to lock up Cyrus and do this restaurant. What will it take?" Sean Parker of Napster, Facebook, and Spotify had visited us a few times shortly before we closed Cyrus and had displayed, in my opinion, a serious desire to be our sole investor in reopening Cyrus.

This call came after *months* of hide-n-seek with Sean and his many layers of staff. I had to wonder why they were finally ready to move forward. The idea of navigating the many layers of lawyers and staff surrounding Sean was not my idea of a reason to interrupt my time with Jakey.

"Tell them you can't find me right now, please," I requested.

I couldn't help but chuckle at the juxtaposition of four billionaires vying for my attention while I was living in shorts and flipflops and playing with dogs for the summer. The beauty and irony of that morning in my truck was that I realized that I already had everything I needed. I had comfortable clothes and cheap, slightly bent, gas station sunglasses. (I don't deserve good sunglasses; I lose them.) I had my two best friends with me, their odor had deeply permeated the cloth seats in my crusty F150, but I didn't mind, but I'll probably pop for the leather next time. I had everything I needed, and I was on my way to play with Jakey. He was my ball-obsessed buddy who I hadn't seen in twenty-four hours.

I was missing him. I didn't need to open another restaurant to make a living. So, this next restaurant venture could be just about wanting to cook for people again, the pure joy of cooking. A sense of peace and gratitude washed over me as I let this thought sink in. I was and am so very fortunate. And there I was—one old truck, four billionaires, thirty minutes. Maybe that should be the title of this book? Aunt Maureen and Dad would have loved this story – except that the dirty, dog-scented truck would have pissed Dad off.

This level of attention from Barbara, Sean, and Sandy was mind boggling. I trusted Barbara's sincerity; she wasn't in this for monetary or personal gain. She was in this for her community. Sean was a bit trickier to figure out. We'd talked so much in the past, so I knew that he shared my passion to create a unique culinary journey. But Sean hadn't made a move until that day. Why then? I wondered the same about Sandy. Why was it suddenly time to move forward? The only thing I could think of was that word had gotten out that I was on *Top Chef Masters*, though it was still a secret that I'd won. Remembering my conversation with Randy and Harriet, I thought the sudden interest could have something to do with my suitors wanting an association with the burgeoning Chef Douglas Keane brand.

The concept of celebrity is a very uncomfortable one for me. I think that there is a variable, unquantifiable value in celebrity power that creates its own niche in any potential deal or relationship. This value has permeated our culture. Chefs are just one of the most recent groups to get the celebrity moniker. American society in particular is so obsessed with celebrity that we manufacture them like dolls. We created TV shows that feature people just going to the grocery store with a TV crew in tow, and we made those shoppers famous just because they were on TV. So, a guy that can beat some starch out of carnaroli rice could just as easily be anointed with celebrity status, right? Makes perfect sense, given these recent trends, but being a *celebrity* still feels weird to me.

Some people literally find me physically attractive because of my chef status. Do you know how hot, sweaty, and grimy it can be in the kitchen after twelve to thirteen hours of work? It's the antithesis of sexy. I'm truly not that good-looking; I'm not in great shape. It feels like the moment my photo appeared in *Food and Wine* magazine or my chubby cheeks sweated it out on *Top Chef Masters*, some women fell in love.

"Can I buy you a drink, Chef? Are you married? Happily? Wow, big shoulders, Chef!"

I wondered whether the billionaires courting me were equally as smitten. I wanted to pause before meeting with them. I'd gotten all the leverage I needed, and maybe more than I felt ready for that morning. I wanted to set aside the thoughts about celebrity and the questions about the uncanny timing of three potential investors calling on the same day within a half hour of each other. I wanted to focus on getting back to the joy of cooking in a positive work environment and the dream of creating a unique culinary journey for people. And I wanted to throw a ball for Jakey. That was a clean transaction; no celebrity status involved. I'd call the investors back later. Jakey was waiting.

I did return the calls, and with Barbara's blessing, I eventually struck a deal with Sean Parker and his team. But five years later and some valuable retrospect gained, it just wasn't meant to be. Unfortunately, pretty renderings were as close as the Sean Parker-Cyrus partnership got to building.

In an article in the *San Francisco Chronicle* after our project was abandoned, Sean stated, "I've eaten all over the world and think that Doug is one of the best chefs in America. He deserves to have a platform that allows him to show the world how extraordinary his culinary vision is. This just wasn't realistic."

I appreciated the comments about my cooking, but I took a little issue with the way the realistic statement was pointed. The end result was that I had to start over. So, I dug deep, harnessed my Midwestern work ethic, and got back to work. Lael and Barbara Banke wouldn't have let me give up on my Cyrus 2.0 vision even if I wanted to, and I knew it. I had a restaurant to build. So, I do what I always do, pick up the pieces and soldier on.

CHAPTER THIRTY-SEVEN

"Waiting For My Real Life to Begin" by Colin Hay

The time between our break with Sean and opening the new Cyrus included what you read in Chapter One, but it also included a brief period before I became dangerously depressed in which I dreamed of a better future for those of us in the restaurant industry. I imagined a life in which I could live my vocation, cook for people to nourish them, and make them happy. And I knew well during that time that I needed to be healthy in this new life. Moving forward, I would need to do things very differently. Actually, we all would.

I sat on the ground with my dogs a lot. I missed Dolly and Maxie, Lola, and Milo, and just the thought of Finnegan and his beautiful crease and happy soul brought me to tears. I lost my best buddy Finn, another bright light, and I haven't recovered. I'm not sure how long the loss will hurt, but I know that when it finally passes and moves to the background, I will cherish my time with him and how he tried to teach me to not complain and to find silliness and fun in every little task during the day. He took his whole life in stride and made me appreciate being in the moment. He left a huge hole in our pack and in my heart. He's also left me with some incredible memories and lessons that will pick me up when I fall deep.

But I had found immense peace with the pack of five rescues. The farm had expanded from just dogs to include two sheep, three goats, three chickens, two pigs, and two calves. It was the best therapy in the world to sit right in the dirt as they slid up next to me and recounted their days to me in baas and moos. Try having a bad day when Quinn, the beautiful, black Baby Doll sheep waddles over and offers a kiss.

I watered my fruit trees a lot, too. We had an amazing orchard at the house that was planted for Cyrus to use. It was gorgeous and full of all sorts of extraordinary fruits. The orchard had an automatic watering system, but off to the side were six types of citrus trees that were initially cast away and languished by the side of the house for a few years. This forest of misfits was close to joining the compost pile when I felt a connection and finally planted them. I watered them every day by hand. And I loved it. I moved from one tree to the next, making sure they got their fill and then back again to remoisten the roots. It took me a lot longer than it should have, but that was the point. It was rewarding to see their progress, and the fruit they produced last season was far more rewarding to me than any star rating could quantify. And it was real.

I dreamed while I watered my trees, and I dreamed when I sat with my pack. My dream was about fixing a broken industry, about all the players in this industry doing some soul searching and finding our path back to true hospitality. In order to heal, we would all need to get back to the core value of people taking care of people. I couldn't think of anything more beautiful in concept than that, even for this unabashed animal lover. But both sides, the guests and the workers, needed to be taken care of for sustainability. And for too long, this industry called *hospitality* had let its own down while only worrying about the guests.

As discussed, we needed to fix the staffing model. We also needed to embrace the technology that already existed for kitchens. There are cooking methods (sous-vide) and pieces of equipment (combi ovens, circulators, vacuum sealers) that allow for a high level of consistency, perfection, and preservation to be achieved with less bodies needed. This technology is currently used in only a few places on the very high end, and at the fast-food segment. Some of it currently gets stuck in archaic, misunderstood governmental red tape restrictions, but it doesn't have to be the reality.

With regard to staffing, there will be a temptation to employ fewer people but pay them the same. But I think that's way too short sighted.

For the next essential step in healing this industry, I knew then and know today that I need your help, because my dream also includes you, the guests and fans of everything culinary. For most of this book, I've pointed the finger at myself, the food writers, the critics, the billionaires, and even other chefs. But if you think that as a civilian you have no culpability, get ready to be in the firing squad. I'm asking you to put your goddamn phones down and enjoy the experience of dining out again. *Please.* Talk to your dining companions. You brought them for a reason, right? Try to capture the moment with your eyes, ears, mouth, hands, and heart instead of with a six-megabyte photo to share with all of your anonymous followers. I know, I know . . . you are driven by the thought that those followers need to know right in that moment that you are eating in the latest and greatest establishment that was just written up on that oh-so-hip blog whose author was bought and paid for by whoring his words for food and drink. *My bad.* And I see you making waitstaff stand patiently by before you allow them to puncture the top of the soufflé with the sauce because you *need* to change to a different filter on your phone camera first. I mean, your elite reviewer status on Yelp could be jeopardized! *Please*, just put your goddamn phone down and eat dinner.

When did we get so far away from human connection, living in the moment, being present, and communicating in person that we needed to move all of our relationships online? The fact that some guests say nothing to the waitstaff who constantly check in on them, but then later put on their capes and let loose online is pregnant with dysfunction. *Oh, my! They put too much salt on the scallops. I can't wait to write about that.* How about this? Before you memorialize the assault on your iPhone, ask the waiter if you could get a refire. Then, before the mind readers in the kitchen viciously attack your next course with the Red Hawaiian Kilea salt, they might be able to adjust the seasoning, and everyone could get what they want. The restaurant could get a happy guest, and you could get an enjoyable meal; win-win. Or is the fear of face-to-face confrontation preventing you from speaking up to your server? If so, I promise you that your honest feedback to a server doesn't need to be confrontational; it can just be honest communication delivered politely.

But wait, you insist, you are going to write *nice* things about your experience. You're helping the restaurant with all of those pictures and comments, right? No, you're not. You are contributing to a core issue that has cancered this industry. You are a match on kindling soaked with gas. Going out to dinner stopped being about sharing a meal with loved ones a long time ago. It's now more about clicks and likes and self-promotion. I guess we all have a need for people to tell us we are great or special. But look where that got me and my chef colleagues Bourdain and Loiseau. That kind of social media toxicity doesn't lead to happiness. It will never make you feel fulfilled, no matter how many likes and clicks you get; you'll just keep wanting more. I don't wish that addiction on my worst enemy, let alone you, my readers, and hopefully my guests in one of my restaurants one day soon.

Here's an alternative to posting about your meal on social media; pull your server aside and tell her how great your lunch was, ask to go back into the kitchen and meet the cooks and dishwashers, and then thank them for a great experience. Maybe even buy them a six pack; it takes a lot of beer to make a great restaurant. Connect with the staff. If that seems too scary at the moment, like coming out of the closet at your confirmation scary, then try writing it down on paper instead of online. Put a real signature and a stamp on it. Drop it in the mail. If the chef or manager is worth half their weight, it will get read at lineup or posted in the kitchen for everyone to appreciate. Or make a phone call and speak to a human; you might just make a friend for life.

I have a dream that at some point in the near future, people will put down their phones, look across the table at their dining companions, and enjoy a meal. It's about being present in the moment and appreciating what is unfolding right in front of you in that very second as opposed to capturing a photo of it to share with those not present. Later, after the meal, you can use your memory to tell a loved one how great that salmon was, or how much fun you and your dad had while enjoying the bottle of wine. But at the table, take a moment and smell the fresh citrus zest releasing its essential oils into the air as the mussels steam in your bowl of soup. Or savor that squish of sweet fat as you bite into your A-5 Wagyu steak. Or notice the tacky, shiny glaze of reduced wine as it coats the short rib. Appreciate the fact that your water glass is full as your server magically floats in between you and your dining companions without ever interrupting your union. See it . . . taste it . . . feel it. Don't shoot it on your phone. It's meant to be right now. That's the point, and I don't want you to miss it. I'll make you a deal; you stop posting about your meals, and I'll stop reading those posts. Come say hi to me and my team in the kitchen instead. I'd sincerely love to meet you.

This time, in my real life, the restaurant experience will be different for me, and I hope for you, the guests, too. I want to cook for you at the highest level in a beautiful building with breathtaking views. With the help of a very motivated team, today, I can finally say that we have created one of the best restaurants in the world on many levels, regardless of ratings. It's about happy people trying to make their guests happy.

CHAPTER THIRTY-EIGHT

"Hunger Strike" (25th Anniversary Mix) by Temple of the Dog

I hope you come and visit Cyrus to experience what my team and I have created. Cyrus isn't just a restaurant. It's a culmination of a life's worth of observations. It's a righting of wrongs and an interpretation of how things can be. It's an idea and a dream that speaks to the *What if?* in us all.

What if you drive up to Geyserville for your birthday with people you love? What if you turn off HWY 128, pass the train tracks, and turn right onto the gravel road? What if you roll down the window to listen to the crunch of gravel under your tires and to inhale the sweet vineyard air? What if, on the exhale, you breathe out your stress and allow the vines to take care of it? What if you allow yourself to feel excited, the kind of excitement that electrifies you and makes you feel a little giddy? What if you allow yourself to embrace a new kind of dining experience, to be adventurous with your pallet, and to let the Cyrus team do the work? You've earned it.

The smell of the dirt in the evening air around the steel canopy entrance to Cyrus offers a foreshadowing of the tastes that await you inside. That soil, the agriculture, is the single most important aspect of our Cyrus home. Our neighbors, the farmers of Sonoma County, grow some of the most flavorful foods in the world, and we foster those products and turn them into your dinner.

To the right of the entrance stands a magnificent plum bonsai. Depending on the time of year, you might see some leaves, buds, or even some small plums. The placement isn't ornamental. The purpose of the tree is to pay homage to the agricultural roots of this land. The Cyrus restaurant building was originally a Sunsweet prunes packing facility, and we wanted to shepherd that connection to the history of this beautiful place.

Nick Peyton, dressed to the nines in a sharp suit, will most likely be the first friendly face you see at Cyrus as he greets you at the door. I begged him not to wear a tie this time around, but when he does, I always smile because part of what I love about him is that he's always done this work his way.

Katelyn, our manager and sommelier, will whisk you into the Bubbles lounge. At this moment, she has twenty-nine things she's responsible for, but the most important one is getting you welcomed.

KP, with her short, bobbed hair tucked just behind her ears, will pour you some bubbles or bring you one of our five seasonal cocktails crafted by our bartender, Isiah, to start your celebration. Isiah, a lanky six foot two, will have been squeezing juices for hours to create the perfect cocktail to ease you into your evening. KP's going to be your new best friend by the end of the night. She can't help herself. She loves meeting and learning about people. When KP looks at you through her black-rimmed glasses with intense concentration, you'll know she's really listening to you because she's genuinely interested.

When Aaron, with his Mandy Patinkin brow and thoughtful smile, delivers your canapés, he will describe each of the five tastes to you. He likely prepared these first tastes and may covertly observe nearby as you bite into the warm gougere with Comte fondue, the star of the salty role. When he's satisfied that you love it, he'll don a sheepish grin and hurry back to the kitchen.

After drinks and canapes, Karla will escort you past the wine cellar and to the kitchen table. With a passion for all things hospitality and getting it right, Karla will obsess about making your evening perfect. But most importantly, she genuinely cares. We all do. A lot. It's because of our love for the craft, love for you, and love for this dream called Cyrus.

If I am lucky enough to welcome you to Cyrus, then I'll have the privilege of meeting you at the Kitchen Table. Cyrus truly is my home, and I love having people over. But it's important to me that you know that I'm not an important factor in your journey at Cyrus. It's you first and then the team.

The evening playlist, always soulful, is likely to include Chris Cornell on acoustic guitar or "She Talks to Angels" by The Black Crowes. I try to utilize the music of artists stripped down to their essence, just as we prepare our courses (about seven, depending on the night) with a respect for the essence of each ingredient in relationship to the others, much like the way music notes work together in song.

Matt, with his long hair tied back in a ponytail, and his thick glasses steaming up from the liquid nitrogen, might be at the kitchen table with me. Ask him a question about the ingredients he used to meticulously build the display on a bed of ice in front of you, and he'll tell you about the people who planted, grew, nurtured, and delivered them. He won't tell you that he's been working since eleven in the morning to make this dish shine for you.

Mauricio's shy demeanor contradicts the boldness of his culinary creations in the most intriguing way. He's the one who will add a splash of liquid nitrogen to the chilled corn consommé with a mischievous grin to jazz it up just before serving. Ask him if he has my water bottle. "You're doing great" is printed on it, and Mauricio likes to take it and place it in front of anyone who might need a little pick-me-up.

Next, please take us up on our offer to walk the kitchens, really. I'd love for you to check out the design and meet the other chefs. I'll likely crack a joke at Chef Drew's expense in an effort to make him smile; poor guy has been laughing at my lame jokes since 1999. Truth is, he's quiet. Unlike KP, Drew will *not* be your new best friend. But he cares more than anyone about making your experience at Cyrus perfect, and he knows more about the ingredients and recipes than anyone in the kitchen. And, despite his shyness, he'll talk with you, unless he's plating an entree. In that case, he won't hear you; he'll be in a zone impenetrable by the best of us.

Take a stroll towards the pastry kitchen and, on the way, you'll get to meet Luis and Cesar in the scullery. Washing dishes and cleaning pots and pans is remarkably tough work, and it's easy to get tired of doing it. But these two masters own their domain like no one else. Two of the busiest and most important pieces of the machine that is Cyrus, Luis and Cesar do the work of four people, and they do it with a steadfast pride that I deeply admire.

Just ahead, you'll find Josh and Anh in the pastry kitchen. Talk about a dynamic duo. They arrive at eight in the morning to make chocolates, breads, and ice creams. They perfect each item until they are satisfied, which doesn't come fast. Don't forget to congratulate Anh on her recent American citizenship. She won't tell you, but I will; she aced the test! It's worth mentioning that most pastry departments in top-tier restaurants are outliers, fringe teammates who keep to themselves. Not at Cyrus. Much of the leadership of our kitchen crew starts with Josh, a true one-of-a-kind professional with a dedication to the enterprise, and to his craft that led him to engage a different restaurant staff dynamic that we all benefit from.

Back at the kitchen table, we'll next serve you the wagyu, the steak from that special breed of cow. The small bite of heaven completes the kitchen part of the journey in a truly memorable way. I won't tell you more here; experiencing it in person should be your introduction to this unexpected and brilliant treat created by Cyrus Schultz, our aptly named beverage director. Schultz is a force of nature fueled by passion; he's never consumed a drop of caffeine. His polished, professional style comes through in his creations. Still, the wagyu, like everything at Cyrus, is a team effort, and you must know that the crispy crust is all Jae's doing. Jae, our extern from Singapore turned permanent employee, can be spotted implementing finishing touches to your dishes in the kitchen. Standing next to Jae will be Gino. Hard to miss at six-four and hair pulled back tightly with a smile big enough to fill the kitchen. As they begin to prepare the next few courses for you, the chemistry and teamwork between these two friends makes their herculean workload seem effortless. That's the point.

Next, Kimberly Beltran will lead you through the sliding glass doors to the Dining Room. Your view of the vineyards through the glass wall will be nothing short of spectacular. The grapes glow in the evening sunlight, as if Mother Nature is an eager member of our Cyrus family. Fun fact. Kimberley is the second generation of Beltrans to work at Cyrus. Her dad was one of our most beloved captains at Cyrus 1.0. Now, Kimberly brings her own brand of excellence to Cyrus 2.0.

Adison or Gabriel, or both, will lead you to your Dining Room table and explain the next few dishes. They will pour your wine, help you navigate other beverages and mark your table settings. Matt, in addition to perfecting the finishing touches to your wagyu, will likely deliver your main courses to you after he helped cook them.

Chefs Josh and Anh, who you met over in the pastry kitchen, will have been waiting all day to serve you the next few courses—cheese and two desserts. Prepare to be blown away by the attention to detail and seasonal thoughtfulness put into each bite. Josh will have obsessed over each and every placement of garnish for three days before unleashing these masterpieces. Desiree and Eve are entrusted to execute Josh and Anh's final vision with love and care. They will plate your final courses and deliver them to you beaming with pride.

While you may not have an opportunity to meet Amber and Chef Londo, as they work behind the scenes, they are another important part of our Cyrus family. Amber, our utility person in charge of reservations, event sales, investor relations, and social media, pinch hits in multiple areas with ease and humor. Londo, or Little Drew, with his military haircut and Midwestern looks, takes care of our production and preparation. He also feeds us our family meal. It's common to see him bobbing and weaving in and out of the kitchens, giving the team a fist bump as he passes.

Is that it? Not quite. A long time ago I asked myself a "What if?" What if we could create an eight-foot wall of flowing chocolate inside a secret room filled with the aroma of chocolate and the theme song from *Willy Wonka*? It had to be done. And now, it's waiting for you. Once inside that secret room, I hope you'll have some fun and pull that phone out finally. Or allow Sean, your chocolate captain, to take a few pictures for you; no selfie stick necessary. But I also hope that you'll look into your dining partner's eyes and tell them you love them. That's what special moments in secret chocolate rooms are for, to celebrate with those who have stood by you. We wanted to create a room where magic happens, and you are the final piece of that puzzle at Cyrus.

Cyrus offers a full journey from start to finish for you, for our Cyrus family, and for me personally. This journey was nearly cut short more than once, and the fact that it's now continuing and gaining momentum with every passing month fills me with the deepest joy, gratitude, and love. I hope you'll feel those emotions at Cyrus and that you'll be able to connect with people you care about and people who care about you in a way that people don't usually make time for anymore. The connection might heal you. It has for me. I hope you'll allow us to create that time and environment for you because I know what it's like to feel disconnected, and I want to be part of the antidote for as many people as I can. Life can be truly beautiful, and I hope you'll let me show you one small piece of that wonderous beauty.

RECIPES FROM THE HEART

Mom's Cajun Shrimp Recipe
(Serves 8)

1lb unsalted butter
½ cup Worcestershire sauce
¼ cup freshly ground and toasted black pepper
2 tsp chopped rosemary
2 tsp Tabasco sauce
2 tsp kosher salt
3 cloves garlic, finely chopped
6 pounds large shrimp (16-20ct) in shell
4 lemons, thinly sliced, seeds removed

Preheat oven to 400F. In a saucepan over low heat, melt the butter with Worcestershire sauce, pepper, rosemary, Tabasco, salt, and garlic. Simmer for ten minutes on low heat to blend the flavors. Arrange the shrimp and lemon slices in a large baking dish, in a single layer. Pour the warm sauce over the shrimp. Place in oven and bake uncovered, stirring once or twice until the shrimp are just cooked through. Approximately ten to fifteen minutes. Transfer to a serving platter and serve immediately. Mom serves it with warm crunchy sourdough to sop up all the juices. And a light salad as the side dish. Don't forget plenty of empty bowls to collect the shells. Or just cover the table in old newspapers and get messy with the shells.

Steak and Mashed Potatoes for Dad
(Serves 1)

For the Steak:
1 thick (1 ½ inches) center cut Prime grade NY Strip steak (16 oz boneless)
2 tbs oil (canola, corn or grapeseed)
Salt
1-2 sprigs of thyme
1 clove garlic unpeeled
1 Tbs Butter

For the Potatoes:
1 lb Yukon Gold Potatoes, peeled and cut into 1-inch cubes
6 oz butter, cold and cut into small cubes
¼ cup milk
Salt

In a small pot of salted cold water add potatoes and bring to a boil. Reduce to a simmer and cook for twelve to fifteen minutes. Drain the potatoes in a colander. While still warm mash the potatoes with a potato masher, a ricer, or a fork. With a spatula push the potatoes through a fine mesh strainer/sieve. Put into saucepan and using the rubber spatula fold the cold butter piece by piece over low heat. Add just a touch of milk to help keep it emulsified and continue to keep warm. Season with salt and serve immediately.

Preheat oven to 375.

In a medium sized cast iron skillet heat pan to high heat. Add one Tbs Oil. Place generously seasoned steak (both sides please) in pan. You want to hear the sizzle. Allow a hard sear to create a crust for about one minute on heat, turn down heat slightly and continue to cook for two more minutes on the same side.

Flip steak over and turn the heat back up for a minute and cerate similar crust on this side. Continue to cook for approximately three minutes altering the heat as needed if it starts to burn the meat. You want a deep shiny golden brown.

Place the steak and pan into the preheated oven for four minutes. Pull steak out and place back on medium to high burner. Add the other tbs of oil. Smash the garlic with your palm and throw it into the pan with the skin of the garlic still on (this protects the garlic from burning), add the sprigs of thyme.

Drop the Tbs of butter into the pan and immediately start to spoon the combined oil and butter froth on to the top of the steak. You are now butter basting. Try to position the sprig of thyme and garlic on the top of the steak and keep basting for thirty seconds more.

Take steak out of pan and let rest in a warm place for at least fifteen minutes.

After resting. You can briefly place it back in oven for three to four minutes to rewarm.

Slice into five or six thick slices and arrange over a heaping spoon of the mashed potatoes. Season steak with a little more salt over the sliced pieces.

Chocolate Chip Cookies with Iced Milk Shots
(Serves 8-10)

For the Cookies:
1/2 cup butter, softened
1/2 cup granulated sugar
1/2 cup brown sugar
1 egg
1 tsp vanilla extract
1/2 tsp baking soda
1/2 tsp salt
1 1/2 cups AP Flour
1 cup dark chocolate chips

Preheat oven to 350 F

Cream butter and both sugars until smooth (three to five minutes in mixer on medium).

Add in egg on low. Add Vanilla Add baking soda, salt, flour, and then chocolate chips. Combine well. Drop small, quarter sized spoons of cookie dough onto sheet pan. Bake for six to eight minutes, (edges should brown slightly). Cookies can be rewarmed slightly before serving for two minutes to give just out of the oven feeling.

For the Iced Milk Shots:
1 qt milk
1 cocktail shaker
chilled shot glasses

Lightly rinse the shot glasses in cold water and place in freezer without drying. Allow to chill for at least fifteen minutes but can be done a day ahead if desired. Place milk in cocktail shaker about ¾ full and place in freezer for fifteen minutes before ready to serve. When ready to serve pull out chilled shot glasses. Place the shaker top on milk in cocktail shaker and shake for fifteen seconds. Pour immediately into shot glasses and serve with warm cookies.

Truffled Red Wine Risotto with Parmesan Broth
(Serves 6)

Risotto
2 sprigs parsley stems
4 sprigs thyme
2 bay leaves
1 tsp Black Peppercorns
1 tsp Fennel Seed
(Wrap tightly in cheesecloth. Secure with butchers twine.)
¼ # Butter
2 cups caranaroli rice
½ small onion, minced fine
1 clove garlic, pasted (with a tsp salt)
2 cups pinot noir
1 qt rich brown chicken stock
6 ounces white truffle butter (or regular butter and fresh truffles at the end)
2 tbs red ver jus
2 tbs parsley, finely chopped
1 tbs chives, minced fine
Salt and Pepper to Taste

In a non-reactive pan. Melt ¼# butter. Add bouquet garni (parsley, thyme and bay, peppercorns, and fennel seed) add onion and garlic. Sweat until onion and garlic are completely soft with no color. Add rice and stir (use a heat-resistant rubber spatula or a strong wooden spoon) to coat evenly with butter. Add wine, season with a little salt, and let reduce until completely absorbed. Add stock several ladles at a time. Continue to add stock until rice is almost cooked through (approximately twenty minutes on low heat).

When rice is just cooked through add all the truffle butter, parsley, and chives and ver jus. Season with salt and pepper and place in warm bowls. The rice should be extremely creamy but still emulsified.

Bring parmesan broth to a boil and add 1 tbs of cold butter and blend with a hand blender. Spoon foam off the top of risotto and sauce around the risotto. Serve immediately.

Parmesan Broth
2 tbs butter
1 onion, small dice
1 leek, chopped (white part only)
1 garlic, head, cut in half
1 fennel, small dice
2 tsp tomato paste
3 sprigs thyme
3 sprigs parsley
3 parmesan rinds
Water to cover

Sweat onion, leeks, garlic, and fennel in butter until soft. Add tomato paste and cook until a fond begins to form on the bottom of the pot. Cover vegetables with water and add an extra inch of water. Add Parmesan Rinds, thyme, and parsley. Bring to a hard boil. Simmer for two hours. Strain through a fine chinois and reduce by half. Season with salt if necessary.

ACKNOWLEDGMENTS

Meghan Davis Hill: Your brilliant coaching, probing and questioning to get more out of me made the process of writing wonderful, necessarily painful at times and beautiful in the end.

Kimberley Cameron, my literary agent, and John Koehler, my publisher. Thanks for believing and investing your time and reputations to get this book out in the world.

Tony Kalyk, a friend for life who helped push the final edits and formatting to submission.

Lael, for being there for eighteen years and giving me the space to write this when I needed it.

PHOTOS

Photo by Cynthia Glassell

Photo by Aaron Leitz

Photo by Cynthia Glassell

Photo by Cynthia Glassell

Photo by Cynthia Glassel

Photo by Cynthia Glassell

Photo by Cynthia Glassell

Photo by Jay Evan

Photo by Jay Evan

Photo by Cynthia Glassell

Photo by Jay Evan

www.ingramcontent.com/pod-product-compliance
Lightning Source LLC
LaVergne TN
LVHW042250070526
838201LV00089B/95